Benjamin Franklin, Thomas Jefferson, and other founders of our nation were deists, supporting the belief that God, once having created the universe, assumes no control over life, exerts no influence on events of daily livings and provides no supernatural revelation.

Another perspective about God's role in our lives is expressed in the following manner: "You are not an accident. Even before the universe was created, God had you in mind, and he planned you for his purposes. These purposes will extend far beyond the few years you will spend on earth. You were made to last forever!" ~ Rick Warren, The Purpose Driven Life.

Who is right?? Why do rational people passionately support one extreme or the other, or countless alternate belief systems? What are the global consequences of our different perspectives? Is there a rational way to align competing schools of religious thought so as to foster dialogue and embrace our similarities rather than our differences?

In The Christian Pluralist: An Invitation From The Pew lay authors John Charles and Bill Buffie seek to give voice to the moderate middle who yearn for modem religions to be more effective in promoting compassion in a world increasingly threatened by competition and extremism. As lay people they offer a unique perspective and provide insights into how those in the pews reconcile the conflicts between traditional doctrine and cultural/moral relativism.

P9-AOJ-369

THE CHRISTIAN PLURALIST

an invitation from the pew

William C. Buffie, M.D.
John R. Charles

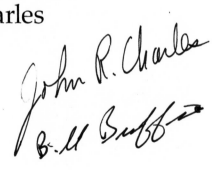

authorHOUSE™

1663 LIBERTY DRIVE, SUITE 200
BLOOMINGTON, INDIANA 47403
(800) 839-8640
WWW.AUTHORHOUSE.COM

AuthorHouse™
1663 Liberty Drive, Suite 200
Bloomington, IN 47403
www.authorhouse.com
Phone: 1-800-839-8640

AuthorHouse™ UK Ltd.
500 Avebury Boulevard
Central Milton Keynes, MK9 2BE
www.authorhouse.co.uk
Phone: 08001974150

First published by AuthorHouse 3/23/2006

ISBN: 1-4259-0832-2 (sc)
ISBN: 1-4259-0831-4 (dj)

Library of Congress Control Number: 2005910872

Printed in the United States of America
Bloomington, Indiana

This book is printed on acid-free paper.

Cover Design and Imaging by Claire Buffie

As one who taught history, I vividly recall lively discussions with young people about how, during particular times, religious belief and resulting fanaticism triggered the most atrocious acts and fired the very hatred that truly religious people supposedly abhor. Sadly, we live in such a time today.

Buffie and Charles provide a timely, thoughtful and balanced perspective about how religious faith, particularly from a Christian perspective, may embrace a diversity of belief. The book gently challenges those convinced of the infallibility of their own beliefs, supporting the often-ignored words of the Rabbi Jesus, "In my Father's house are many rooms."

The term "important reading" is bandied about ad nauseam, but if ever that description were appropriate, it is appropriate for this book.

Dr. H. Douglas Williams
Superintendent,
Metropolitan School District of Perry Township
Indianapolis IN

Buffie and Charles have had the courage to share their misgivings about the direction taken by many Christians in denying authenticity to the religious searches and beliefs of others. They have set out a discussion to assist these fellow Christians to be open to and embrace others who believe differently than they do. They invite all to join in the work of creating a global community of religions and religious persons dedicated to the peace and common good of humankind.

Judith C. Wimmer
Professor, Religious Studies
Edgewood College, WI

The Christian Pluralist challenges us not to rethink our faith but to question our approach toward other faiths. The authors, William Buffie and John Charles, maintain that the core of Christianity lies in tolerance and understanding, and that true Christians – indeed, people of all persuasions who are true to their faith – should therefore adopt a tolerant and understanding approach toward other religions.

Buffie and Charles express their argument eloquently and persuasively. Theirs is a voice of reason, acceptance, and compassion in a world that is, increasingly, influenced by religious absolutism, intolerance, and extremism.

Clayton Bond, Business Executive

DEDICATION

To our families and fellow spiritual seekers

ACKNOWLEDGEMENTS

Many have shared this journey with us and we so appreciate all the support, comments, criticisms, and words of encouragement as the ideas for this book have evolved. Especially we would like to thank the early readers of our first drafts – Moe, Kim, Pat, Ed, Mark, Chris, Kevin, Fred, Bill, Clayton, Rosie, Joyce, Gary, Roland, Sandy, Doug, Jason, Joel, Bob, Teri, Scott, Daryl, SUMC Fellowship of Seekers Class. The many hours of discussion and perspectives shared have shaped our path in fruitful and fulfilling ways.

To Craig Potter, chair of the English department at Perry Meridian High School, and Bill Orme, associate librarian at Indiana University Purdue University at Indianapolis, we owe special gratitude for their editing assistance, commentary and encouragement. To Dr. David Bodenhamer, executive director of The Polis Center in Indianapolis, we are indebted for his taking the time to review later drafts and excerpts and helping us to refine our style in a manner that we hope will speak to a large audience. To Dr. Judy Wimmer, religious studies professor at Edgewood College, and Dr. John Buenker, history professor at University of Wisconsin-Parkside, thank you for helping us to sharpen our focus on our target audience and for encouraging us to go forward with offering the lay person's perspective on pluralism. To Dr. Tom Davis, Religious Studies Chair at Indiana University Purdue University at Indianapolis, and Tim Shapiro, president of The Indianapolis Center for Congregations, for the time you have taken to critique our final manuscript and provide encouragement as we have reached this pivotal juncture in completing our work, we are very grateful.

Finally, our families have read and reread numerous sections of our drafts and helped us maintain our drive and ideals. Our wives, Donna and Jo Ellen, most importantly, have never wavered in their support of endless discussions through the development of this project and our collective spirituality.

PREFACE

Our culture seems awash in all things religious. <u>The Da Vinci Code</u>, by Dan Brown, is a worldwide phenomenon. Rick Warren's book, <u>The Purpose Driven Life</u>, is not only a blockbuster bestseller; it spawned an entire industry of follow-up media materials. *The Passion of The Christ*, Mel Gibson's movie about the crucifixion of Christ, sparked intense interest and debate among Christians and non-Christians alike. <u>The Five People You Meet in Heaven</u>, by Mitch Albom, is still on the bestseller lists after more than a year. Recently aired on *Larry King Live*, three clergymen, a spiritual writer and an atheist debated heaven, evil and the existence of God. A New York Times article, titled *U.S. Christian Conservatives Take Aim at Filibusters*, described a program called "Justice Sunday, Stopping the Filibuster Against People of Faith." "People of faith" are rapidly becoming major political players.

Many pundits say "moral values" decided the 2004 U.S. presidential election rather than the economy, the war in Iraq or any other controversial issue. These same pundits say "moral values" is code for anti-same-sex marriage and anti-abortion positions, and these subjects are religious to their very core. More and more frequently politicians are questioned about their faith and religious convictions as a condition for their acceptability as candidates. President George W. Bush is the most overtly religious president in modern times and that includes the "born-again" Jimmy Carter.

While this religious "awakening" can elicit many positive results, it can also foster hostility and divisiveness. It seems that, in many cases, instead of bringing us together, religious fervor is tearing us apart. Within and beyond our country's borders there is deep division over whose God is the "true" God or whose doctrine the "true" doctrine. We hear religious leaders denouncing other faiths or other belief systems as the work of the "devil." Religious extremists quote the Bible, the Qur'an or some other sacred text to "prove" that God endorses their words or deeds. We see young people in the Middle East using their bodies, strapped with explosives, as weapons to kill the "enemy" and themselves in the name of God. Conservative Christian Broadcaster Pat Robertson called for the assassination of a foreign head of state on his television program. A Jewish fundamentalist assassinated Prime Minister Rabin in 1995 because Rabin dared to attempt peace with the Palestinians, the "enemy".

Religion plays a major role in the cycle of violence and terror we witness all around the world. Muslim fights Muslim, Muslim fights Christian, Christian fights Muslim, Jew fights Muslim, Jew fights Jew, Christian fights Christian, and on and on. One question repeatedly asked is, "Does it have to be like this?" Are religious people required to view people of other faiths or people of no faith as competitors or enemies? Isn't there a better way to practice one's religion? These questions led us to the search that ultimately produced this book. To us, there seemed to be a disconnect between the religion practiced in the pews and the religion we read about in the newspapers. Using the Bible, Qur'an and other religious texts as weapons with which one faith system could prove its superiority to another just did not fit our religious experience and practice.

We began our search for another perspective with discussions among our friends and members of our church. We wanted to know how others felt about God, truth, and orthodoxy. We read numerous books, articles and tracts. We listened to radio broadcasts. We watched interviews and documentaries on television. We attended lectures. We explored the idea that no one system of belief owns the ultimate "truth" about God. We came to believe that each of us has the ability to experience God and religion in a very personal and unique way. Therefore, if one understands religious truth in a relative sense, then there is no justification for using religion to propagate hatred or competition. To borrow from the beautiful John Lennon song, *Imagine*, …if there was no orthodoxy, there could be no infidel, if there was no heresy there could be no heretic to blame or vilify. If no one owned the exclusive path to God, no one could claim God as the source of his or her prejudice. Imagine.

CONTENTS

Many cultures contribute to the richness of our world community. Just as every culture has time-honored traditions that make its heritage unique, each of us has individual qualities and characteristics that make us special. Let us learn more of one another...in knowledge there is understanding; in understanding there is respect; and where there is respect, growth is possible.

The Master Teacher, Inc.

INTRODUCTION

For everything there is a season, and a time for every matter
under heaven: ...a time to embrace, and a time to refrain from
embracing; a time to seek, and a time to lose; a time to keep, and
a time to throw away...

Ecclesiastes 3.1

We live in a world of sometimes-frightening religious polarization.
Fundamentalists illustrate the extreme manifestation of conflicting
agendas, but potentially even more alarming are the battles ongoing
in political and social arenas of those claiming moral superiority
based upon their culturally determined interpretation of scripture.
A division is growing and is fostered by those who try to reduce
extremely complex issues into simple moral imperatives, using their
God, or their interpretation of God's thoughts, to support particular
agendas. Conservative traditionalists presenting their understanding
of God's intentions in very simple terms are, in some respects, doing
a disservice to all of us. Unless we all seek to understand *why* we

believe what we believe, there will continue to be absolute claims that will necessarily contribute to further polarization and conflict. None of this is simple. To suggest that the understanding of God's message can be simple if only we are obedient to the dictums of one's culturally determined faith undermines the potential that we see in a more pluralistic approach to matters of faith. Leaders who promote their messages in simplistic, rigid, or exclusive terms are, we fear, behaving irresponsibly in an age of multi-faith communities, locally and globally. There is a time to refrain from embracing solely our own perspective, a time to relinquish claims of absolute insight into the mind of God, and a time to re-evaluate whether the message we promote can, and should be, more inclusive. That time is now.

This book is the product of years of searching, of asking of ourselves many unanswerable questions, but also of faith in the process of evolution -- evolution of individual growth, religious thought, and the relationship of humankind with one another and with God. It is written from the perspective of what we believe to be a relatively large number of people, both churched and unchurched. These are lay people searching for answers not in absolute terms, but in ways that promote acceptance and diversity. It is written not by those with formal training in theology or philosophy, but by two of us who are moved by the searching of our fellow seekers. As members of Southport United Methodist Church in Indianapolis, we are fortunate to be part of a community of spiritual seekers wherein no subject is taboo, with discussion fostered on sensitive subjects by lay leaders as well as our pastors. Discussions over several years concerning controversial theological issues have left us impressed by how many members, previously perceived as part of the traditional status quo, entertain questions similar to ours. Rather than questioning whether we, with some of our "heretical" ideas, belong in our church, we find ourselves empowered to give voice to the unspoken thoughts of many who share similar uncertainties.

If we are successful in delivering our intended message, however, we hope it will not come across as heresy in any sense. Furthermore, it should not be construed as superior or more enlightened, but rather as only a testimony to what is, and always has been, part of the human consciousness -- the need to ask questions, challenge the status quo, push the dialogue. Others have professed ideas similar to ours but sometimes, to our dismay, in a manner that implies or blatantly professes superior insight, with an attitude that is condescending toward traditionalists and quickly creates a schism that is difficult to bridge. Such an attitude suggests a linear progression of individual and societal intellectual and spiritual growth, each step more advanced and superior than its predecessor. There is an arrogance that comes across in this attitude that is an impediment to reaching our goal of simply promoting dialogue amongst religious communities that might lead to respect and acceptance of alternative perspectives rather than fostering the defensive reaction that so often characterizes discussions of this nature. Rather than a linear progression, we would suggest the process is more circular. The path of our journey is not a line but an arc, part of a circle that never actually has an endpoint, or final revelation. Instead that circle is intersected frequently by others also searching, but on a different paths. Together, all of the circles, spiritual paths, form a sphere with countless points of intersection contributing to the whole. It is this awareness of the value of each point contributing to the whole for which we strive. As the interaction of our thought processes necessarily occurs at widely varying stages -- the character of which is determined by *current* experience, reason, science, and faith -- it should be no surprise that conflict is inherent to the process. Conflict and competition however do not of themselves necessitate winners and losers -- for collectively we all have something to gain from shared experiences, even if we draw different conclusions when confronted with the same question.

What began as a series of discussions trying to clarify our own beliefs, then writing down some ideas so as to more clearly communicate our thoughts with our families, has now evolved to the point of wanting, not with just a little trepidation, to share our convictions with a larger audience. The cynic in us tells us we will be ignored or dismissed by those entrenched in their beliefs, but the idealist, the optimist in us, hopes to spark a groundswell of discussion, not necessarily just in academic circles or seminaries, but amongst lay people. If the dialogue, with its promotion of acceptance and diversity, is close to the heart of what we suspect to be a significant number of people, then it will require of our leaders -- both religious and secular -- a paradigm shift. Lay people may effect change in academic circles, but their voices must be heard.

James Hollis, in <u>The Middle Passage: From Misery to Meaning in Midlife</u>, challenges us to constantly ask of ourselves, "Who am I, apart from my history and roles? What work needs to be done?

What am I called to do? ...we are judged not only by the goodness of our heart, but also by the fullness of our courage." It is in this spirit that we offer a common person's perspective, challenging our leaders to ask of themselves the same questions Hollis asks of us as individuals. Can we make this world a more compassionate place in which to live? What work needs to be done? Do we have the courage to break down the barriers confronting us?

This is not a book about theological answers, but rather a book about questions. It is a book about how we deal with questions. It is a book about understanding who we are and why we are incapable of consensus concerning final revelations or truths. It is a book about making choices, with our options being products of new insights and new possibilities. It is about challenging traditional doctrine, but at the same time preserving the timeless truths carried by our various traditions. It is a book about understanding the standards by which we judge issues of theology and moral authority. It is a book about inclusion rather than exclusion. It is a book challenging the wisdom of either/or propositions, with the suggestion that we will be better served if we re-direct our energies in search of those qualities and goals we share in common. More importantly, God too, we believe, will be better served as well.

In the course of raising many issues, we will share our personal opinions and beliefs, but we cannot emphasize strongly enough from the outset that we are not trying to convince the reader to adopt our particular theology. Certainly there are some points that we hope the reader will embrace, but these are primarily matters of attitude relative to understanding one's personal perspective that we feel are desirable to facilitate the dialogue. We believe it to be extremely important in reading this book for the first time that one not succumb to the natural tendency to formulate arguments against opinions offered which may differ from one's own. Energies spent being defensive will cause the reader to miss some valuable points, points which may in fact soften the potential offensiveness of some of our opinions. Granted, this is a lot to ask of any of us. We are all guilty of being poor listeners, tending to formulate responses in our minds all the while nodding our heads in affirmation of the other, when in fact we are listening without hearing. But we recommend that this book be read several times, resisting the temptation the first time to have the red attack pen in hand, but have an open mind, open to just trying to understand another viewpoint. We do not expect agreement, only dialogue. We know from sharing early drafts of our manuscript with a variety of people at many different places on the continuum of religious and spiritual thought that many opinions we share touch sensitive chords and can indeed be potentially threatening to individuals passionate about their beliefs. One cannot promote a discussion of this sort without eliciting a protective reflex response from the passionate reader. We expect and fully endorse the anticipated dialogue of respectful disagreement. We welcome the expected criticisms and critiques to follow. If such discussions take place, then we will take it as a measure of success in achieving one of our primary goals.

We offer this book furthermore as an invitation to lay people to become engaged, but even more so to those in the pulpit. Statistically, the traditional church is on the decline in terms of global membership, but we see a tremendous opportunity for leaders of our churches, mosques, and temples to reach out to those who find themselves disillusioned with the current religious climate. There is tremendous growth potential for church communities that seek to understand and reach out to the many spiritual people who currently maintain a good distance from traditional religious venues. If our religious leaders read carefully and with empathy, an insight may be gleaned that may change how traditionalists choose to relate to those outside the walls of the religious mainstream.

As we explore this opportunity in the ensuing chapters, we hope to develop a line of reasoning that might allow others to understand why we are committed to a pluralist philosophy. Pluralists believe that there are a wide variety of faiths that all are legitimate, and contain valuable truths, when considered from the proper cultural perspective. Though it is most certain that all will not agree with our conclusions, we hope there will be, at least, an appreciation for the rationale involved. We want to share with the reader our struggle to reconcile apparent contradictory truths. We know our perspective to be a common one amongst the spiritual unchurched as well as those who define themselves as part of the more traditional church community. We also know that many clergy struggle with many of the same contentious issues we will discuss. We strive to provide justification for an evolving worldview amongst lay people and clergy, one that expands the role and reach of Christianity without undermining it. While the specifics of our discussion most directly confront traditional Christian perspectives, we hope it will be obvious through the course of the book that the same arguments may be directed at any others that may promote an exclusive theology.

The first chapter will describe the overarching Christian Pluralist perspective, with the rest of the book describing our journey to reach this particular viewpoint. The second chapter will frame the discussion further, describing our background and history leading up to this effort, but also preparing the reader for that which will follow. Chapter three will explore the stages through which we mature as individuals and examine parallels with the evolution of religion, for understanding our own biases will be essential if one is to have an open mind to what will follow. Just as we as individuals must rely on some sources of authority in dealing with the practical realities of life, so must our religions do the same. Understanding how authority achieves its position, particularly as it relates to the Bible, is the focus of the fourth chapter. The fifth chapter delves into the key issue of truth. How do we define it? Who determines it? Are conflicting truths reconcilable? If authority and truth can be seen in a different light, then how might an expanded understanding of God translate into our everyday life? Chapter six will offer a description of a world subject to a God inclusive of, but not limited to, traditional religious constructs. The seventh chapter will examine the commonalities found amongst world religions and celebrate the opportunity to share them. In the eighth chapter we will acknowledge the limitations of all of our perspectives, but encourage us to not shy away from uncertainty, but rather embrace it as a healthy by-product of the inquisitive mind. We will offer our own personal beliefs, recognizing that we are just at a single point on a continuous journey, and put forth practical suggestions for how the Christian Pluralist philosophy may be translated into social action. Each chapter will be followed by discussion questions that may be useful for introspection and/or small group discussion.

Embracing diversity however does not mean abandoning one's individual faith. It does not mean we have to combine all the different traditions into one watered-down, anything-goes universal faith. We believe we can embrace others and still be passionate Christians, just as we hope Muslims can embrace Jews and still be passionate Muslims, and Jews can do likewise and still be passionate Jews. We don't want to change the worship, lessen the importance of Jesus or any of the great prophets, or deny their messages. We simply encourage Christians to examine *why* they are Christian, *why* the Muslim is a Muslim, and *why* the Jew is a Jew and so on. As we have progressed through this journey, it has been gratifying to discover how many efforts are currently being made to embrace the interfaith experience, but it still is developing with an "us" and "them" mentality. Likeminded "liberals" gather to promote our similarities, but to those in mainstream churches, mosques, and synagogues we are still subject to our culturally prescribed more limited perspective, trying to keep it simple so that none of us will be confused by the multitude of perspectives that may put a chink in the armor of the status quo. Please keep an open mind as we offer justification for expanding our perspective and experience with "others." It is our contention that there is justification for our leaders to take a new approach to such issues, in the hope that we can be joined together by our spirituality, rather than separated by religious labels and doctrine. Religion can be healing rather than divisive. To make it so however requires a conscious choice, and it is anything but simple. Our plea to our religious and political leaders is to figure out the end game and then to accept the challenge of confronting tradition, *choosing* to create an empathetic and compassionate mindset that truly values the experience of others. Tolerance of the perspective of others is simply not enough. We have an opportunity at hand now to make new choices based upon all of our collective experiences, scriptures, faiths, and reason. Centuries ago it was a select few who could assimilate the multi-faith experience, but the current global information age offers broader horizons for all. Truly embracing and accepting -- not just tolerating -- the perspective of others creates an entirely different attitude from which point issues of a contentious nature can more likely be resolved in a civil manner.

We are truly indebted to the many friends and family who have endured countless hours of discussion, without which we never could have achieved our current degree of clarity with respect to our own beliefs. Your criticisms and encouragement have been invaluable, as we have progressed through the high and lows of trying to put our ideas down on paper. For all of your love and support, we humbly thank you. It is only through many meaningful discussions with all of you that we feel empowered to share these ideas with others.

DISSCUSSION QUESTIONS

1) Will I ever reach an endpoint in my spiritual journey?

2) Are my beliefs culturally determined? If not, how?

3) Should the beliefs of the laity influence the message from the pulpit or is it a one-way street where matters of theology are concerned?

4) Do I see or hear of people disillusioned with organized religion? If so, why are they disillusioned?

5) Is religious competition harmful? Are interfaith experiences desirable?

6) What role do I think religion should serve? In my life? In society? In the world?

CHAPTER I

THE CHRISTIAN PLURALIST

Pluralism: The belief that no single explanatory system or view of reality can account for all the phenomena of life.

The American Heritage Dictionary

Somerset Maugham, in <u>The Razor's Edge</u>, describes the spiritual journey of Larry, the central character who returns from WWI disillusioned with western high society life, abandons the comfortable and predictable lifestyle afforded him and strikes out in search of the meaning of life. His travels take him to India where he receives wisdom and insights from the guru Ramakrishna Swamis who, on the subject of God, advises, "A god that can be understood is no God. Who can explain the Infinite in words?" The narrator (Maugham) later asks of Larry, "But how can a purely intellectual conception be a solace to the suffering human race? Men have always wanted a personal God to whom they can turn in distress for comfort and encouragement." Larry answers the traditionalist question saying, "It may be that at some far distant day greater insight will show them that they must look for comfort and encouragement in their own souls. I myself think that the need to worship is no more than the survival of an old remembrance of cruel gods that had to be propitiated. I believe that God is within me or nowhere." Salvation, according to Hindu tradition, may be achieved by way of love or works Larry learns but "...the noblest way, the hardest, is the way of knowledge, for its instrument is the most precious faculty of man, his reason."

Citing Larry's journey is not meant to suggest that the traditional Christian should be swayed into thinking that love, works, and knowledge are the keys to salvation rather than God's grace. Though many may share this philosophy, others, not just Christians, reasonably reach different conclusions. The point though is that all of us, in reaching some finality with respect to our spirituality and faith, must ultimately rely upon our ability to reason. Christians, just as is true for those of other faiths, must decide what role scripture plays in the decision-making processes. Do reason and experience determine how we interpret scripture? Or does scripture in and of itself determine how we are to reason? If so, what makes one religion's scripture more valid than another?

These verses from The Second Letter of John in the New Testament give us some idea as to how the fundamentalist Christian, committed to the infallibility of the Bible, might react to Larry's philosophy:

Many deceivers have gone out into the world, those who do not confess that Jesus Christ has come in the flesh; any such person is the deceiver and the antichrist! Be on your guard, so that you do not lose what we have worked for, but may receive a full reward. Everyone who does not abide in the teaching of Christ, but goes beyond it, does not have God; whoever abides in the teaching has both the Father and the Son. Do not receive into the house or welcome anyone who comes to you and does not bring this teaching; for to welcome is to participate in the evil deeds of such a person.

What a disconcerting edict to promote Christian isolationism! Does this type of teaching reflect what mainstream Christians believe today? If so, then we are indeed in trouble. The religious landscape will always be cluttered with the destructive "us versus them" mentality. If not, then perhaps this is an example of scripture that needs interpretation relative to cultural context (much more on this in a later chapter). Perhaps the author of this New Testament passage felt such exclusive urgings were necessary for the survival of a fledgling religion, but is this the message Christians now want to send to one whose spiritual journey finds a home in a "competing" school of thought?

As we share a number of perspectives gleaned from literature, historians, professors, philosophers, theologians, clergy and our own personal beliefs, many questions will surface that we realize come across as threatening to conventional or traditional Christianity. Despite our trying to anticipate and allay such feelings in a preemptive fashion, it has been quite a struggle trying to accomplish this. Some with whom we have shared early drafts of this book came away with the impression that we were anti-Christian, or at least that the tone of the book was too confrontational with orthodox Christianity. It is worthwhile to address this sentiment directly now so as to understand how this occurred and perhaps try to convey our thoughts in yet another manner. To alter the tone of our writings in major fashion, however, we feel would deny the passion that we have experienced in putting our thoughts on paper. Somehow, in speaking to a significant part of what we hope will indeed be part of our audience, we may not always successfully navigate along the fine line that divides challenging the *reasons* people develop particular beliefs versus coming across as being critical of the actual *beliefs*. To be critical of the final beliefs or faith of others would be totally in opposition to all the points we promote for embracing diversity and pluralism. To the contrary, we think we understand and do not wish to take issue with the basic conclusions, though not necessarily the rationale, the orthodox Christian (or any believer) has reached through pursuing his or her faith journey. Our plea though, as will be emphasized throughout the text, is for such individuals to ask of themselves *why* they believe as they do.

Consider these reactions from a variety of individuals with whom we have shared various drafts of our manuscript:

"You have a great idea, one that is much needed in our country."

"It transcends Christianity."

"I think that your book is inspired and inspirational."

"This is an idea whose time has come."

"Your book is offensive to Christianity."

"A more tolerant world would not necessarily be better."

"You don't address the problems associated with eliminating faith as we know it today."

"You made specific efforts to mention points of agreement with traditional orthodox Christianity, though there are still some parts that may be offensive."

"The truth is you are making moral claims, but you have no real authority other than your own preference."

"Reason...demands complete moral anarchy without central authority."

"You present a boundary-less God."

"Your ideas do make so much sense, but how can I preach such a message from the pulpit without compromising my orthodox roots and expectations of my congregants."

"If you are going to argue for the evolution of God and religion to traditionalists, your argument had better use scripture as its basis."

"I do not think that the ideas you present are likely to be a solution or an answer in the way I think you want them to be. I accept that I can never know why the universe is here, how it all began, whether there is a God (I think not). I just do not see that human intelligence is capable of revealing this (certainly not in my life-time) and I cannot just believe it because of faith. In this sense I guess you'd call me a rationalist; I don't want to spend time trying to prove what I feel is 'un-provable.' Neither would I think it reasonable that a God (if he/she/it did exist) should expect mankind (with all our differing cultures, languages, and existence at different evolutionary points) to come to a belief in one system and accept that as the truth to the exclusion of all others. So in a way I guess I have a problem with any religion that seeks to evangelize because I don't see how it could logically set itself above any other."

Common to all of these reactions is the fact that they are entirely predictable if one knows the bias the reader had before reading the book. We feel compelled to respond directly to some of the issues and attitudes presented, but please realize that we will not at any point suggest that we "eliminate faith as we know it today." Our position is one that advocates *validating* the faith of devout believers, not eliminating it. Certainly some have rightfully pointed out that there is an overall tone that forces traditionalists into a defensive posture in reacting to our thoughts. However, it should be clear that our questioning the rationale for beliefs should not be construed as attacking the beliefs themselves. We ask of the devout believer that one take a new look at conflicting opinions, and we think we provide ample rationale for questioning any rigid dogmatic perspective, without demanding agreement. Orthodox Christians should not feel singled out, as it is the *absolute* and *exclusive* beliefs of *any* individual discussing matters of the spiritual realm that we seek to bring into question.

We believe it is reasonable to validate the faiths of all, if the spiritual journey is understood in relative terms, subject to critical evaluation incorporating experience and reason, and understanding cultural bias. We hope and expect that evangelizers within any faith would present their beliefs in a different manner, would be more accepting of diverse opinions, if they were rigorous in critically evaluating the basis for their own beliefs. In so doing the deeply religious individual might better be able to defuse the "us versus them" mentality that exclusive revelation fosters, and that is counterproductive to the goal of "wholeness." There are two spheres in which we strive for this wholeness -- the internal and the external.

Internally, we cannot help but be affected by our attitudes about religion. If we feel our perspective is superior to all others and that anyone who believes in another path to God is somehow lost or outside the blessings of God, we are inevitably isolating ourselves from those others. This attitude affects us even if it is just at a subconscious level. We see manifestations of this phenomenon in many exclusive organizations. Fraternities, sororities, country clubs, political parties and many others demonstrate both the positive and negative aspects of exclusivity. Even when the whole reason for the organization is to make the world a better place, like service organizations and churches, we see an attitude of the "us versus them" mentality. It is an inevitable outgrowth of believing that there is one revealed answer to a very complex and mysterious question. Members of these organizations can work with "outsiders," socialize with them and even profess love for them, but they can never feel "whole" with them. The difference may be subtle, but is significant.

Externally, the well–intended service organization may inadvertently isolate itself from those whom they are trying to serve, and this dynamic too should be recognized. The givers, although trying to expunge the appearance of exclusivity, can never quite escape the isolating effects that are an inherent part of any exclusive organization. For centuries Christians even exported their theology by the sword. Followers of Christianity demonstrated open hostility toward people of other faiths. Leaders exhorted their followers to remain separate from the "infidel" or "heathen." It is a very recent development that Christians are backing away from this sort of aggressive isolation. Christians are beginning to reach out to the others and apologize for past persecutions. This is a positive development, but we need to go beyond acknowledging past sins. We need to expand the boundaries of our faiths.

Each spiritual seeker must have faith in that which resonates with them after deeply reflecting upon all criteria relevant for that particular seeker's journey. But does such an attitude leave us with a God without any boundaries? Do we subject ourselves to a world of moral anarchy if we question man's acquiescence to a scripturally determined absolute authority? Is morality just a reflection of our own preferences? We don't think so. The common bonds that unite diverse religions all seem to reflect some basic human values that are universal in nature. As theists we conclude that these principles are in fact a reflection of God's ubiquitous nature, regardless of culturally determined doctrine. If in fact God does not exist, then man's entire spiritual journey has been an intellectual and philosophical exercise not based in reality but in response to serving man's needs, i.e. to provide comfort and understanding and also to avoid moral anarchy. If God does not exist, then man has actually shown himself capable of generating a moral compass through his own process of rationalization. This is not a criticism. If God does not exist, then it is just our reality. The point is that with or without God, we have developed boundaries. With or without God, chaos does not reign. Scripture, if not actually God-inspired, must be recognized as a reflection of man's eternal struggle with his own human nature -- the battle of good versus evil. One might argue that if we knew that God did not exist then the whole landscape would be altered, and we would have to start the argument anew. However, since we can never prove the existence or nonexistence of God, the discussion in this regard is moot. Therefore it is reasonable, in a practical sense (recognizing fully that *our* practical sense may differ from that of our rationalist agnostic or atheist friends), to embrace the premise that God does indeed exist. Defining God's nature however is not so simple, and this will be one of the main issues addressed in the book -- what do each of us *know* about God, versus *believe* about God.

The next to last comment noted above, as offered by one of our clergy friends, raises an interesting question relative to this discussion. Can we offer a scriptural basis supporting our position? We believe there are many passages in scripture that complement our discussion, but to try to use scripture as the final "authority" in an appeal to those entrenched in orthodoxy would be inconsistent with our concerns relative to the role of scripture for any of us on our faith journeys. Though we will cite examples from the Bible, the Qur'an, and the Bhagavad-Gita that are universal and inclusive in scope, others may offer more exclusive passages, or interpretations thereof, that lead us back into conflict. If each of us values our own perspective, ranging from a traditionalist's exclusive claim to the one true way versus our inclusive pluralist approach, how do we find an answer to this dilemma?

A "Christian" approach to this apparent paradox offers us an answer. Scripture -- whether talking about the Bible, Qur'an, or others -- we believe assumes a variety of roles *depending upon the listener.* Scripture, following in the Christian tradition of considering Jesus simultaneously human and divine, may be 100% divine to some, yet 100% humanist to others. We propose that tradition, experience, and reason all influence the weight assigned to scripture by any of us as individuals. This seems to be stating the obvious, but it is an important concept to acknowledge if one has the desire to reconcile conflicting truths. Granted, the acceptance of this paradox leaves a great many ethical dilemmas still to be contentiously debated, but at least a new mindset frees us to learn from other traditions without giving up our own. Arguments will remain, but if we value the other's tradition, we are more likely to find common ground.

Scripture of all kinds can speak to different people on different levels. We are not all required to live by blind faith in conflict with those whose reason and experiences lead them to another faith. Ours is a reasoned faith, but our reasoning, and therefore our assignment of scriptural authority through faith, is no more valid than that of others subject to traditions and experience worlds apart from our own. If we choose to approach the competition amongst religions with humility, then accepting the paradox allows us to embrace and truly accept others as equals. To exercise our free will and make this choice, we believe, is the ultimate manner of worshipping God. To do so is to reach the pinnacle of truly living the Golden Rule as expressed by all religions. The unwillingness to give up claims of exclusivity proves to be, more often than not, self-serving (well intended perhaps, but self-serving nonetheless).

We are not alone in questioning traditional interpretation of scripture. This is an evolving process and we don't think it should threaten traditional Christians. After all even Jesus re-interpreted Old Testament scripture to put it in proper context for the times. Uncertainty regarding the issue of absolute authority should not be perceived as a negative, especially when the absolute cannot be verified. It is not a retreat, but an advance, to acknowledge and embrace the uncertainty. *We don't become less Christian when we affirm the experience of others; we become more Godlike.* The simple beauty of many inspirational scriptures is that of being timeless. Scriptures of "conflicting" religions interpreted through reason and experience appropriate for the historical context prove to be adaptable living traditions whose survival depends upon their evolution. Where might this evolution take us? What will be the role of each religion? Is it a contradiction in terms to offer a description of the contemporary Christian Pluralist?

Through its concepts of the Holy Trinity and the death and resurrection of Jesus, orthodox Christianity has the potential to play a unique role in leading the evolution of global religions to a more accepting approach to one another. Consider this perspective offered by Father John Dourley in <u>The Illness That We Are</u> as he explores the problems associated with competing monotheistic religions: "In the face of this problem, Christianity, with its central symbol of death and resurrection, could be the candidate among the monotheisms to break this impasse and to affirm itself by transcending itself -- to die in its present configuration in order to rise in some form of more inclusive consciousness. It might do this by coming to see itself as one, but only one, significant and very valuable realization in history of the psyche's drive to express the full extent of its religious import. It could then more humbly confess its partiality and seek missing aspects of its potential wholeness in the religious experience of other traditions, or in direct dialogue with the source of all religious experience -- the unconscious within each individual." As theists we suggest that the "unconscious within" is actually God. Our religions are unique products of God's presence manifest in particular cultural contexts. We don't see Christianity however as needing to die in order to become more inclusive, but instead envision it as transforming and extending itself.

We would like to propose that one can *choose* to apply the Christian concept of the Trinity in a universal religious sense, not just as an explanation of the nature of God. Traditional Christianity, we believe, is but one of three points of the spiritual triangle. God the Father is one point. Judaism and Islam share the conceptual point of a father figure handing down authority, giving guidance, and commanding respect. God the Son, manifest by Jesus Christ, occupies the traditional Christian point of the triangle. Co-existent, and equal with the other two points, is God the Holy Spirit. This Spirit may be manifest in a multitude of ways, in secular as well as religious realms, unlimited by particular doctrines. This is inclusive of all spiritual journeys. We think this is the Spirit of Truth referred to by Jesus in the Gospel of John. We think it is the source of compassion of the Buddhist. We think it is the Absolute Reality, or Brahman, for the Hindu, the truth and freedom that transcend all. If the orthodox Christian does believe in God manifest as three separate entities simultaneously, and Jesus Christ having lived a life 100% human and 100% divine, then it is not unreasonable to suggest that God's nature, and the path to salvation itself, if truly available, might be revealed by three (or more) mechanisms simultaneously. Does relating primarily to one point on the "God triangle" preclude truly embracing the other two? Is any one point more important or valid than the other two? We don't think so. The perspective of the Christian Pluralist embraces a new paradigm, accepting the paradox of seemingly contradictory human religious interpretation being transcended and united by God's universal presence. If we don't recite and believe each line of the Apostle's Creed, does this mean that we are not Christian? Did God or Jesus identify the defining criteria for Christianity, or did humans do so? If human, should such definitions be immutable? Does one definition fit all? By the end of the book, we hope each reader will have been motivated to search deep within to try to answer these questions.

Struggling to clarify our own beliefs and wanting to share with others has simmered under the surface for years; however, it reached the boiling point a couple of years ago when Rick Warren's book,

<u>The Purpose Driven Life</u>, took the American religious community by storm. Embraced as a model of inspiration and understanding by churches throughout the country, it has become the best-selling hardback in U.S. history. Our church also promoted his philosophy from the pulpit and in book studies. We were supposed to receive comfort from his assertions: "You are not an accident. Even before the universe was created, God had you in mind, and He planned you for His purposes. These purposes will extend far beyond the few years you will spend on earth. You were made to last forever!" But for many of us there are just too many inconsistencies with this philosophy for it to provide much comfort. How many times have any of us heard the sole survivor of a horrible accident say, "I just want to thank God for protecting me and my being alive"? What about the pregnant mother and her three children who did not survive? Think of how their family must feel hearing the survivor giving his or her personal testimony as to the benevolence of God on the evening news.

Many simply cannot believe that there exists a God that is the architect of all that is good and evil, directing who may live and who may die, when and where. Many believe that natural laws decide why one may die and another may live, rather than God "having a plan" for each of us. For many of us there is more comfort in the belief that God's presence in all moments helps us cope with the unimaginable, or that which seems intolerable. Consider if the accident survivor instead said, "I'm thankful to be alive but I can't imagine the hurt the other family must feel this moment. My faith in God will help me through this somehow and I can only pray for others that calling on God's presence might help them as well." This would demonstrate empathy and is a message of healing. This response of "I want to thank God..." whether it comes from the accident survivor or the winner of an athletic contest is a learned response. It comes from religious leaders oversimplifying the personal nature of one's relationship with the divine. It turns off people who are struggling with the role of religion in their lives. If that is what God is all about, many have no interest in the further pursuit of that relationship.

Many other scholars, just as learned and passionate as Rick Warren, have come to different conclusions as to how God interacts with humanity. Benjamin Franklin and Thomas Jefferson, offer the deist belief that God is like a great watchmaker. God is thought to have wound the clock and then became uninvolved; He then allowed life to unfold driven entirely by natural law without any divine intervention. How do we decide which, if any, of various heartfelt opinions are to be given credence? Why was the Christian community so fanatical in its endorsement of Warren's book? Trying to balance and interpret such viewpoints along with so many questions of our own led us to offer a response to those who are so dogmatic in their approach to matters of religion.

Rick Warren, when interviewed by Larry King, attributed the success of the book to its simplicity. We cannot help but feel however that there are too many complexities relative to Christians' role in society that have been largely ignored by such a book. We think passionate Christians can and should present their perspectives couched in terms that don't oversimplify an exceedingly complex subject. The simplistic inspirational model fosters an air of exclusivity amongst noncritical believers that separates them from those of different faiths. Movies like *The Passion of The Christ* stir emotions that further confrontation and division. Our hearts ache to see and hear individuals and churches compete with one another claiming to understand God in any absolute terms. If such books and films were presented with proper acknowledgement of their own biases, then they could take their appropriate place as testimonies to the complex experiences of their authors. We want to share with the reader why it hurts us so to witness both religious emotional outcries and rationalist's decrees presented in absolute terms and how we believe it to be possible to reconcile strong emotions with science and reason. To do so we must critically question the basis for our beliefs. The rest of the book will share our reasons for questioning absolute beliefs whether presented in complex or simplistic terms and where such contemplation may take us.

Discussion Questions

1) How does my ability to reason interact with my faith?

2) How is my relationship with others affected if I only tolerate their viewpoints as opposed to truly accepting them?

3) Is there a universal moral code? What is the evidence? Does it require the existence of a deity?

4) Is the role of scripture subject to my experience as a reader?

5) Does the concept of the religious trinity make sense to me?

6) If God has planned and orchestrates the most minute details of my life, with what theological conflicts am I then presented?

CHAPTER II

FRAMING THE DISCUSSION

Reason, ruling alone, is a force confining; and passion, unattended, is a flame that burns to its own destruction.

Kahlil Gibran

Passion and prejudice govern the world, only under the name of reason.

John Wesley

We share similar backgrounds having been raised in Indiana attending traditional Christian churches with our families. Both of us strayed from organized religion during our college and postgraduate years and didn't feel a sense of void, as we were busy planning our careers and married lives. As each of us began our own families however, our wives were instrumental in encouraging us to find a church home in which to raise our children. Recognizing the value of a Christian upbringing and the sense of community we desired led our families at different times to Southport United Methodist Church, where our paths would eventually become intertwined, and we would develop many of our closest friends. Our church was everything we wanted with respect to raising our children, but gradually, as we independently became more critical in our listening to messages from the pulpit or in our study of the Bible, we found there to be many things that just did not seem to make good sense to us.

With backgrounds of history (John a history major at the University of Southern Maine) and science (Bill a biology major at Northwestern University; medical school and internal medicine residency at Indiana University School of Medicine) we found ourselves questioning conventional doctrine. Many aspects of our religious experience we found to be in conflict with our professional lives and study. Self-conscious of our own hypocrisy in reciting creeds we did not believe, it was easiest to ignore the conflicts, lament to our wives in private, and just enjoy our church community without ruffling any feathers. But to continue to deny one's emerging passion can be unsettling. The thought of just riding out the church years until our children were raised and then drifting from organized religion again seemed cheap and unfair to a community and organization for which we had come to have so much respect. At the same time though, it then became more difficult to find that our belief in much of what was being taught was waning, while we still would take great pride in our church doing so many good things for those less fortunate in this world. Reaching middle age we each began to take inventory of our own spiritual questions and eventually "came out of the closet" to one another admitting that we had difficulty with much of what had been part of our traditional upbringing. More and more we would find ourselves "translating" sermon phrases, creeds, and scripture to make them consistent with our developing worldview. Others, we would soon discover, shared many of our questions. Our study and readings along with this recognition further energized us to try to make sense out of our own emerging philosophy, but at the same time we did not want to abandon our Christian traditions or our church family.

Our allegiances though were further thrown into disarray during the summer of 2003 when books such as If Grace Is True and The Purpose Driven Life became focal points of book studies through our church. Passionate opinions offered by the authors raised many questions spanning the liberal and conservative extremes of Christianity. We didn't want to be disruptive, but we could not deny the passion we too were feeling at this point. We found ourselves going public with our questions, and it felt right. This is a great credit to our pastors and fellow church members. To be able to share our thoughts and still feel welcome was a very freeing experience. But we wanted to do something more. By this time we had traveled far enough on our own journey to be convinced that there was more to this whole Christian story than that with which we had grown up and continued to hear from our mainstream Methodist church. We had the sense that one need not feel hypocritical sitting in Christian pews having the audacity to think impure postmodernist pluralist thoughts! Though this felt right to us, could we actually justify it to others? Could we understand it ourselves? Where might it lead us?

Convinced that this world would be a better place if our common bonds were not overshadowed by those religious conflicts that serve to separate people of differing spiritual perspectives, we embarked upon writing this book. We believe that societies that embrace diversity and celebrate common ground have much to learn from one another. The dialogue, though punctuated by disagreement on specific issues, fosters the empathic listening needed for resolution of conflict. We realize many will question whether our goal of acceptance of other religious traditions as partners in the search for God is worthy of the struggle we propose. We understand that some will wonder if this acceptance will in fact ease tensions among nations, cultures and peoples across the globe. We admit that acceptance is not a panacea for the world's problems, but we firmly believe nurturing a different attitude of acceptance can lead to a higher level of understanding and cooperation amongst the diverse people of the globe. Lacking true acceptance however, lines of division naturally develop on several levels.

On the individual level, we share the assumptions of Father John P. Dourley outlined in The Illness That We Are when he states that Christians *want* to be integrated with the rest of the world, but "Christianity impedes, rather than contributes to, the historical and psychological development of mankind -- if we accept the contention at the basis of Jung's psychology, namely that becoming whole is the ultimate value and goal of the history-making psyche." We know that sounds harsh, and the author did not mean to deny the positive contributions Christianity has made to the world. His point is that the "us versus them" mentality fostered by the belief that Christianity is the sole path to God causes both subtle and plainly overt impediments to real understanding and integration among religions.

Many adherents of "exclusive" religious traditions try very hard to remove these impediments. They contend they can work and live with and even love those who do not believe as they do. We see examples of this ecumenical movement across the world, but even with this effort barriers still exist. Believing the souls of others are doomed for their lack of belief in certain religious doctrines inevitably affects these relationships. John witnessed this phenomenon in his own family. His parents were not particularly religious in his early years. His father did not attend church very often, and when he did, he did so reluctantly. His mother attended more often, but she did not take an active role in John's religious education. His grandparents though were a different matter altogether.

John's maternal grandparents attended a very fundamentalist church. They believed in the "literal" truth of the Bible to the extent that they would not allow musical instruments in the worship service because they could find no reference to them in the early Church as recorded in the book of Acts. Sermons dealt with who was saved and who wasn't. Members were told that anyone who did not believe as they did and did not worship as they did were lost to the bliss of spending eternity with Jesus. A great deal of time and effort was spent trying to determine exactly who was going to heaven and who wasn't.

Wonderful people as they were, they treated John with great kindness and love, but they were very firm in their commitment to support the beliefs of the church. In later years this caused John some concern when he met and became friends with people of other Christian denominations who did allow instrumental music in the worship service. In particular, it was puzzling to realize that one set of grandparents thought the other grandparents were doomed to spend eternity in hell. John spent a good deal of time with his father's mother, and she was every bit as kind and devout as his maternal grandmother. Both women loved God and tried to live good Christian lives. How could it be that one was going to heaven and one was going to hell because her church had an organ playing music as part of the worship service? It just didn't make sense that God would judge eternity based on an organ. Now, in fairness, he knew that the organ was not the deciding factor in the minds of most members of his maternal grandparent's church. What mattered to them was the strict adherence to Biblical dictates *as interpreted by them.*

How could his mother's parents not ache for his father's parents, feel pity, and perhaps even frustration and irritation for their stubborn refusal to "see the light" and take the necessary steps to ensure their salvation? Furthermore, how must the excluded ones feel toward those who feel they are condemned to hell? How did John's paternal grandmother feel knowing that members of her own family thought she was lost to Jesus and that she was going to spend eternity in hell? It must have caused great pain and resentment and a feeling of isolation. She took her religion seriously. The Charles family struggle is just a microcosm of the global struggle amongst competing religious beliefs.

Further to the extreme of the religious spectrum, there are those who, unfortunately, even make a conscious effort to separate themselves from the other. They tell their children not to associate with people of different beliefs. They take great pains to isolate themselves from the Muslim, the Jew, Hindu, the Buddhist, the atheist and even other Christians who profess subtly different theologies. This isolation is guarded jealously and affects all relationships. We believe this attitude does impede our ability to become whole. It prevents us from reaching out and understanding and cooperating with the other. It inhibits the formation of relationships and sense of community so vital to reducing and perhaps eliminating tensions arising from distrust and suspicion of the unfamiliar.

Viewed globally, this "us versus them" mentality can be truly frightening. We see ugly manifestations of such religious conflict all over the world. One religion can more easily demonize another if it feels God endorses its actions. If the only face the enemy has is "infidel" or "Christ-killer" or "barbarian," then how easy it is to continue the cycle of violence. Putting a face on the enemy and entering into relationship with the other based upon trust and mutual respect has the potential to drastically reduce the impulse to violence and hate. How differently would "we" see "them" if we felt all passionate spiritual seekers were on one of the many acceptable paths to God?

Again stated, our goal in writing this book is to give voice to those people who wish to go beyond the current culture of insisting upon the exclusive truth of one religious tradition over all others. The voice of the moderate middle is often unheard as moderates, yielding to the uncertainty inherent in the perspective from which they approach religious matters, often lack the passion to aggressively promote their own beliefs. We seek to give clarity to the thought processes of those who may find themselves floundering in the sea of battles amongst highly passionate religious and philosophical experts who so dominate the religious landscape. The time has come for those of us in the moderate middle to suggest that our leaders pull us back from the precipice of religious pride and conflict. Our leaders need to know that we can still be in relationship with God without being threatened by conflicting experiences or opinions. In fact, we embrace conflict and the dialogue that ensues. Don't shield us from the passion of others. We need to share such passions. We need to understand where they originate, why reasonable people may have different worldviews, and we need to go beyond tolerance and truly accept them. It excites us to think of the possibilities raised by entering into worship side by side with those whose experience leads them down a path different from our own.

In giving voice to the moderate middle, we do not want to exclude those at either end of the religious spectrum. We believe there is ample justification even for the practical atheist to endorse the positive role religion can play in reaching for the common good. Furthermore, there is just as much justification for the devout believer to embrace and celebrate diversity within religion. If we can make a strong case supporting these beliefs, then we feel all of us may be empowered to progress beyond theory and philosophical arguments and venture into the practical reality of dealing with conflicts in a world of diverse, but increasingly interconnected, segments of global society.

Central to this discussion is an understanding of what criteria we each use in determining our beliefs. What factors form the foundation of our faiths? Is faith a gift from God? Once we have faith, how does this influence our interpretation of scripture? If faith is a gift that we must choose to accept or not, then are we referring to faith in the actual existence of God? Is it a gift of faith in one particular religion or doctrine? Would God only offer one gift for all? The entire theological discussion, we must recognize, is muddied from the beginning because *there are no universally accepted criteria* from whence to start. Our cultural biases determine what criteria we use to judge new ideas, thereby prejudging the eventual conclusion. None of us can escape this, and nor should we necessarily try. An awareness of this fact, however, will serve us all well in discussing controversial matters.

The atheist demands that criteria of absolute logic and empirically verifiable facts be met in order to consider the worthiness of any belief. The staunch believer on the other hand accepts the experience and witness of respected predecessors as a valid basis for one's developing set of beliefs. The atheist will argue that this is too subjective and that each generation simply passes on the mistaken prejudices of one's elders. In the religious context it would be suggested that such prejudices are born of the imagination and rationalizing powers of humans in search of answers for questions involving the spiritual realm. Believers, on the other hand, feel that they do in fact *experience*

God on a daily basis. This type of experience, though, is alien to the atheist deeply entrenched in the scientific approach to such matters. The atheist may find it difficult to relate to, or take seriously, the spiritual experience. But should the mind always trump the heart in matters where the imagination or feelings are involved? Such widely divergent starting points leave little reason for those on opposite ends of the spectrum to enter into discussion. But where would science be today if scientific hypotheses were not seasoned with proper aliquots of imagination? Giants of scientific discovery have credited others, noting that they only see with clarity because they stand on the shoulders of others who have had the vision to pursue ideas before they ever could be verified or even considered logical by the prevailing state of knowledge. To shut the door on dialogue just because one's own criteria for belief are not met robs us of the richness of worlds unknown, some of which, though not consistent with the status quo, eventually may prove to be true. Practical reasons to enter into dialogue will be evident if we ask of ourselves the following questions. Are we happy with the direction we see the world heading? Is the practice of religion a source of conflict? Why do I have one set of criteria for belief, yet others, of equal intellect and sincerity, relate to a different set? Am I so certain that my way is the only right way so as to preclude entering into community with the other? Can religion be a vehicle for healing? Can I as an individual make a difference?

After asking ourselves these questions, others naturally followed. Is it possible to put an atheist in a room with a conservative Christian theologian for a discussion about religion and have each leave the room accepting the perspective of the other, truly valuing the dialogue, without feeling threatened, and not needing to defend one's own opinion and experience? Is it possible for competing religions to embrace the "truths" of others without compromising their own commitment to God and their own traditions? Is it possible to juxtapose traditional religious doctrine with more universal principles and still be intellectually honest, remaining true to one's faith, not just rationalizing to avoid conflict? Is it possible to enter such discussions with a mindset that makes these not just possibilities, but probabilities? We believe positive answers to these questions are essential if we are to progress beyond our present state of unhealthy religious and cultural enmity and competition. So much of our feelings of alienation from each other are grounded in our differences: racial, economic, educational, sexual orientation, or religious. But instead of fueling the tension, religion could indeed be a vehicle of healing across these other lines. Instead of providing the haters with divine endorsement, believers could use the power of God (or atheists could "use" the power of religion) to disarm them and make their claims of being God's soldiers empty and hollow. As stated earlier we believe that competing religious *truths* and claims of religious superiority are preventing us from realizing organized religion's true and healing potential. Arguing about the nature of God and divine revelations prevents us from fully manifesting the way of life we would consider to be most god-like. Others have suggested, and we would like to support, the idea that perhaps too much emphasis is placed on the nature of the Giver rather than the most important gifts of key messages of sacred scripture, those of

29

timeless value, having practical application for all who would study them.

Furthermore, it is our belief that there can be no consensus with respect to any ultimate, irrefutable proof of the existence or the absence of God. This is one point on which many theists as well as atheists might agree. Staunch conservative Christian leaders such as Josh McDowell and Thomas Williams in <u>In Search of Certainty</u> contend that there is no empirical proof of either extreme because "the ultimate absolute cannot be proved because if it could be proved, it would not be the ultimate absolute. It would be only a conditional standard in need of validation by a deeper, self-evident truth, which would actually be the ultimate absolute.... If you have any belief at all -- whether it is religious faith or atheistic naturalism -- look deeply enough beneath it and you will find the assumption of an unproven absolute." They go on to argue their conviction that ultimately reason and experience will lead one to conclude that belief in God makes more sense than the alternative.

Lee Strobel though, in <u>The Case For Christ</u>, argues that in his opinion the *evidence* itself is undeniable supporting the Christian tradition. However, in summary he defers to the reader to draw one's own conclusion based on study of the evidence, stressing the importance of at least pursuing the spiritual journey.

Methodists are taught that their Christian faith is a gift from God, which once accepted, is then supported by tradition, reason, experience, and scripture. Scripture in this setting is said to assume primary importance as it transcends any self-serving rationalizations that may be manifest through the other three.

We reference these paths to passionate belief at this point simply to illustrate how sincere, educated individuals committed to Christ came to their ultimate faith through significantly different lines of reasoning. For Strobel the evidence itself was compelling and undeniable, yet for McDowell and Williams the same evidence was not conclusive, but weighing all factors together *their* reason and experience found the alternative to Christian belief to be untenable. For others their faith, once accepted and experienced, yields the inescapable impression that the authority of their scripture is self-evident, though this requires certain assumptions that make such conclusions anything but self-evident. It is obviously difficult, and perhaps impossible for many of us, to put our own reasoning on hold long enough to just listen to new perspectives. Already we have made statements with which many may take issue. We will try to explain our line of reasoning further as the book unfolds, but as we share our thoughts please continue to be open to just exploring with us how we came to this point.

As our own pastors also have pointed out, *all* theologies eventually break down under deep enough scrutiny, but this does not mean they are without merit or truths worthy of examination, or in fact belief. Without simple answers beyond question however, all of us eventually turn to reason and experience to define our beliefs (Once an individual has had a faith experience or defined one's beliefs, then scripture may assume an elevated position). But as any of us go through this process, we believe it is our responsibility to recognize the origins and limitations of our own reasoning if we are to ever understand and value the reasoning of others. We find ourselves in a rapidly changing world of globalization whereby conflicting theologies are evolving side by side with integrating economies, internet mass communication, accessible international travel, and newfound individual freedoms. How we choose to reconcile conflicting theologies will go a long way toward determining the harmony with which globalization takes place. Religious barriers, being man-made constructs, offer the possibility of man-made solutions.

Many have shared with us their frustration with the protective tone of those defenders of exclusive religious tradition that serves only to alienate others, which demeans and devalues the experience of others, which discourages questions and dialogue, and which serves as an impediment to religious acceptance and peace. As lay people witnessing history repeating, we wonder why our political and religious leaders are not able to break free from the shackles of narrowly focused doctrine, to foster true dialogue demonstrating an appreciation for the plight of others. Certainly some believers within various religions are so devout in their beliefs that they justifiably question our basic premise that the world would be a better place if we embraced diversity and were more accepting of other doctrines. Committed Christians or Muslims, we understand, may sincerely believe that the world would be better off and God would be best served if all converted to their respective religions. One has to respect this level of passion and commitment. It is our belief however -- and probably few would argue this point -- that this will never occur. This being the case, where do we go from here? Can one justify being passionate about one's own beliefs, but at the same time be committed to supporting the passion of one who holds to conflicting doctrine? Beyond generalizations and philosophical goals already stated, why should the devout allow any questioning of one's roots steeped in exclusive tradition? In the ensuing chapters we will detail why these questions became so problematic for us, and why we think even the most devout can relate to our struggles.

In trying to put forth a cogent argument promoting acceptance and diversity, we hope that those comfortable with where they are on their faith journey will feel validated, yet at the same time freed to accept and embrace the choices of others, whether it be in regard to matters of faith or other individual freedoms. Those in search of new answers to old questions will feel empowered to continue the search in a manner that does not insult, demean, or patronize those with conflicting belief systems. Religious "truths" no longer are understood as statements of fact which are either right or wrong, but rather we find comfort in accepting Stephen Covey's explanation of how, "we see the world, not as it is, but as we are -- or, as we are conditioned to see it." Covey describes this phenomenon in secular terms, citing universal principles that are part of the human condition. Rabbi Harold Kushner in <u>Who Needs God</u> addresses the issue from the perspective of loyalty to our traditions stating that "religious claims are statements of loyalty rather than historical fact...can be true at a level other than the factual one. Religious claims can be true the way a great novel is true. It teaches us something about the human condition... ."

James Hollis, again in <u>The Middle Passage: From Misery to Meaning in Midlife</u>, expands upon the concept of our being conditioned to view the world in a biased way noting that "when we are born we are handed multiple lenses: genetic inheritance, gender, a specific culture and the variables of our family environment, all of which constitute our sense of reality...families transmit their vision of life from generation to generation..." and most importantly, "just as we see some aspects of the world through any given lens, so we will miss others." This book continues to have a profound influence on our lives as we deal with relationships not only on a personal level, but also as our theology unfolds. Though a difficult read in many respects, it was well worth the many hours we spent dissecting it in our book club. Nine hours of in-depth discussion helped us understand the responsibilities and choices we face in relating to spouses, children, co-workers friends, and our spiritual search. Our time could not have been better spent.

The limitations associated with one's individual perspective is illustrated by the old Indian folktale about six blind men charged with trying to characterize the essence of an elephant, an animal too massive for any one of them to engage all at once. The first blind man, feeling the side of the elephant, declared it to be most similar to a wall. The second, feeling the tusk, described it to be akin to a spear. The third, happening to grab the moving trunk, was adamant in his assessment of it being a large snake. The fourth, feeling the coarse and wrinkled knee, was certain he was touching a type of tree. The fifth, touching the elephant's ear, recognized this to be a fan. The sixth, grasping the tail, declared it to be very much like a rope. Though each of the men spoke loud and boisterously relating their experience and reasoned opinion as to the nature of the beast, none truly knew the total essence of the animal. Only through the collaborative efforts of all the blind men could any of them hope to approach anything that might resemble a complete revelation as to the nature of the elephant.

As religious tradition transmits dogma from generation to generation, much of the tragedy we see lived out on a daily basis results from being blinded to the perspective of others. Just as adults trying to successfully navigate through the middle passage must "acknowledge the partiality of the lens we were given by family and culture," so are we at a point in the evolution of religion where our church leaders stand at a crossroad, facing the realization that they too have a *choice*. Will they choose to acknowledge the lenses through which they view religious matters, through which the roots of their faith take hold, and how these factors affect their teachings? We cannot separate our faith and beliefs from our set of life experiences. In light of our current state of knowledge and experience, we believe it is no longer desirable or appropriate for us to "press on with no faith in our own understanding and nothing but faith in the Truth [i.e. the Bible] that is too great to be diminished by our feeble minds and too great to not transform us" (Christian songwriter, Rich Mullins). The transforming truths of scripture are truly timeless in application to our daily lives, but interpreted through the lens of one's limited human experience the entire richness and fullness of the transformation can never be complete. Our spiritual journeys should always be works in progress.

We have matured psychologically, spiritually, and in our relationships as we have embarked upon this journey. The development of this book has mirrored our own evolution. Early drafts were lacking in empathy for those committed to the status quo and overall had far too much of a negative and challenging tone, but they did generate a lot of fruitful discussion that has provided a springboard for our further efforts. Our own biases and misdirected passions became readily apparent. Our early writings contained "passion, unattended" which, as Gibran has suggested, would have "burned to its own destruction." Taming our passion, and listening in more attentive fashion to those whose opinions and experience contrast with ours, has helped tremendously on our journey. We believe we are more effective writers for having had this experience.

Practicing empathy in the religious context has had effects well beyond our spiritual search though. We find ourselves to be more effective in dealing with relationships on a personal level. Whether it be Bill dealing with patients and families in crisis at the hospital, or John working with impoverished clients trying to ferret out disability issues with a government agency, learning to see an issue from a perspective far removed from our own natural tendencies is invaluable for those of us who truly want to compassionately help the other get through difficult times. We practice empathic listening because we care. We are good at it because we are not trying to help the other by demonstrating *our* rationale, but rather we seek first to understand their thoughts and try to help them on terms appropriate for their particular circumstance, in a manner that will provide comfort for those in need. It's not easy. Some people when stressed can be simply irrational, but are we helping them cope with a difficult situation if we try to force them into *our* rational thought process before they are ready? Delivery and timing become so important when dealing with individuals on sensitive matters. The same holds true as we discuss matters involving religious conflict.

Striving to understand what motivates those with whom we interact has contributed to the personal growth that has strengthened our resolve to advocate similar principles of engagement for matters of religious competition. Our prayer is for divine presence, regardless of what form God may take, to be a guiding force in what we think, say, and write. We hope that this presence will be a source of comfort which will be felt by our readers even in the midst of some ideas which otherwise might shake the foundation of traditional faith. Please be open to the unlimited possibilities engendered by believing in a truly omnipresent but mysterious God; a God who was present before there were Buddhists, Hindus, Jews, Christians, Muslims, or atheists, and will remain present long after all of us are here no longer; a God who may defy human definition; a God who, for reasons which perhaps will never be fully understood by us, may challenge us with conflicting *truths*, the interpretation of which are products of cultural bias.

Discussion Questions

1) Do I believe all of the Bible and traditional creeds to be literally true?

2) If yes, then how do I ignore or attach less significance to some directives in the Bible? On what basis?

3) Do I think the world would be a better place if emphasis on common bonds replaced religious competition? Am I concerned by the direction I see the world heading?

4) Are the views of moderates well represented in the national debate on moral values?

5) Can the "evidence" in support of belief in God stand on its own, or is the interpretation of all evidence affected by my experience, reason, and traditions?

CHAPTER III

UNDERSTANDING BIAS --
GIVING UP CONTROL

We should know what our convictions are, and stand for them. Upon one's own philosophy, conscious or unconscious, depends one's ultimate interpretation of facts. Therefore it is wise to be as clear as possible about one's subjective principles. As the man is, so will be his ultimate truth.

Carl Jung

As newborns entering this world, we are totally dependent upon external help for our nourishment, safety, growth, sense of belonging, and understanding of the vast unknowns that await us. We accept as authority parents who introduce us to a world colored through the lenses of their collective experiences. Ego-driven and self-centered as children, we are oblivious to the perspective of others outside our realm of experience. The safety and security of our comfortable childhood relying on external authority -- parents, teachers, preachers -- establishes a foundation which will necessarily be shaken as we stumble through adolescence, questioning authority but all the while still seeking or receiving external rewards or punishments which re-enforce certain types of behavior. Reaching adulthood, however, we find ourselves immersed in relationships trying to understand and explain our failures and successes in dealing with spouses, co-workers, children, and parents. We gain a sense that our personalities are indeed products of a very complex set of life experiences, some obvious and easy to understand, but many subliminal, subconscious, but real nonetheless. Relationships become understood in a new light and take on new meaning as we understand the extent of the factors which may influence who we are or why our significant others may see life so differently than do we. Developing and preserving healthy relationships requires insight into the process but also a commitment to not project our personality or perspective onto the other. Indeed, embracing those parts of the other which may add to our wholeness, broaden our horizons, and confirm for us the value of empathic listening enriches the relationship. No longer threatened by differences of opinion, but rather understanding the origin of such differences, we can commit to explore together an expanded world, a fuller consciousness, and a richer depth to our being. But this doesn't come without its challenges and uncertainties. It doesn't come without necessitating compromise as we reach impasses, clinging to our own stubborn traditions, while at the same time wishing to discard some of the psychological baggage of our formative years, which we know cannot be healthy for current relationships. With understanding and compromise, though not necessarily demanding agreement, comes peace. At this point in our maturation as individuals it is important that we acknowledge and fully understand the basis of our choices as we interact with others.

Evaluated critically, we may not be particularly proud of some of our choices but at least we gain some insight into their origins. With this awareness we can accept ourselves, as well as others, for who we are but also take on renewed responsibility for who we will become, for our future direction is a matter of choice. From a position of heightened self-awareness, we are no longer dependent on an external system of rewards and punishment, but find that we all have within each of us that which is necessary for wholeness, the realization of which can only be accelerated and enriched by embracing the perspectives of others with whom we are in relationship. Acknowledging our potential however brings with it the burden of responsibility for current choices. Our past has shaped who we are to this moment, but it is our current conscious choices -- fully cognizant of the rich panoply of past and present experiences affecting these choices -- that determine our future.

This process of individual maturation is explored in detail in <u>The Middle Passage: From Misery to Meaning in Midlife</u> by James Hollis, a Zurich-trained psychologist and Jungian analyst. As we studied this book a few years ago, it not only offered profound insights into ourselves as individuals, but we found there to be parallels with the evolution of religion which are quite striking. If we as individuals are capable of understanding the depth of our being -- both inherently good and bad qualities -- and the attendant challenges associated with the knowledge thereof, then can we not expect the same of modern religion? Is it possible, and in fact entirely reasonable, to understand current religious doctrine as an outgrowth of past experience with God, but at the same time recognize the future of religion now should reflect our understanding of God in light of new circumstances and knowledge? Some say God never changes, and that may be true, but certainly our perception of God does. We will discuss some of these changing perspectives as they relate to the Bible in Chapter IV. Whether acknowledged or not, we are constantly revising and re-evaluating God in light of new experience, knowledge, and reasoning. Resisting change and ignoring current experience in order to protect the status quo have been not only doomed to failure, but indeed have been the root of needless harm and prejudice in each generation. As individuals we can accept the victim mentality and be captives of our past, or we can make the conscious choice to blaze a new trail. So it is for society today. Our religious leaders have a choice. Is our future to be solely determined by religious dogma, which is a product of limited human experience? Are we so confident that God's hand, rather than man's desires and needs, was so clearly the sole architect of all that evolved and was recorded as scripture that there is no room for further discussion and interpretation commensurate with current experience? If we believe this to be true, does it hold up under scholarly and moral scrutiny? Or is our God, whom we profess to believe is not limited by time and space, also the architect of our present experience, revelations of science, and philosophical insights, pushing us to another level of consciousness?

Since the dawn of human consciousness we have struggled with questions of spirituality: our origins, the meaning of life, the afterlife, the existence of God, the nature of God. Religion is the natural offspring of the search and is universal in its occurrence thereby implying that its mere existence fills a basic human need -- the need to try to answer many timeless questions and to be connected. In its infancy, given limited knowledge, with the provision of comfort and assuaging fears of the unknown being the primary needs, religion took the form of polytheist beliefs in mythological gods and goddesses. As our scope of knowledge and experience broadened, such religious beliefs could no longer be defended and eventually would become obsolete. Other cultures continuing to explore our place within the universe developed monotheistic religions, while still others emphasized issues of morality without invoking the existence of a personal deity. Within individual cultures "enlightened" leaders fulfilled the role of parental authority providing comfort and direction for the masses, but the comfort provided by a parent begins to break down when confronted with the barrage of new experiences and questioning perspectives, which are so much a part of maturation and adolescence. Though we recognize and appreciate the wisdom of our parents, we have the need to find our own way and to develop our own internal moral compass consistent with *our* set of life experiences. Each generation's unique set of life experiences necessarily will differ remarkably from those of the previous generation.

Challenging religious dogma often involves frank rejection of traditional sacred beliefs, much as a child may reject parental values, and such rejection fosters feelings of apprehension and disrespect amongst those in authority, be they parent or religious leaders. With tradition being threatened and generations of experience and belief seemingly being discarded, the natural instinct is to become protective and defensive. How many times as parents do we take such rejection personally, respond defensively, and contribute to escalating conflict by failing to recognize the same growth experience shared by each generation? As a religious community is our reaction to the natural evolution of new questions from succeeding generations any less defensive? We hold on to traditions that provide us structure, comfort, and direction and want our children to benefit from the same, but not surprisingly, there is no such orderly transition from one generation to the next. Each must find one's own way. Though we may reject the absolute authority of our parents in the process we eventually find that, if our parents did a good job based on sound principles, they have provided us a roadmap, a moral framework that we are able to use as a basis for our own foundation of beliefs. Our beliefs must be consistent though with the lens through which we see life. As parents we struggle with being true to our own values, but at the same time knowing we cannot project or force these values upon our children. Anyone who has experienced the challenges of parenting knows this to be true and sadly also knows the emotional turmoil created by trying to impose our "truths" upon our children. When we reach the point of being comfortable with offering our values and experiences to our children to aid them in their journeys but at the same time not finding it a personal affront when our children make different choices, then we empower them to think for themselves, benefiting from the knowledge of their ancestors, but not encumbered by our prejudices or any sense of guilt we might instill by defensive reactions to any challenge of our authority.

As a religious community so also we see absolute authority being rejected, and we see the struggle between those trying to maintain tradition and those seeking new answers more consistent with the knowledge and experience of a new generation. The struggle, though often bitter, may seem justified in the minds of parents or religious authorities who wish to spare their underlings from the often painful mistakes of youth; authorities whose feelings are further bolstered by their belief in final revelations and God-given absolute authority not to be challenged lest we topple onto the slippery slope of moral decline which might accompany deviation from tradition. Rick Warren, in The Purpose Driven Life, states it this way, "God doesn't owe you an explanation or reason for anything he asks you to do. Understanding can wait, but obedience can't....Obedience unlocks understanding." How we wish it were that simple as parents; won't our teenage children find great comfort in knowing "obedience unlocks understanding"?! As parents we can certainly relate to this perspective and know that with discipline and obedience our children could avoid a lot of pain and mistakes, but as young adults they crave explanation and understanding in a realm different from their parents. It will no longer suffice to say as parents, "...because I told you so." Obedience in a sense becomes negotiable.

History demonstrates that blind obedience is not without its dangers. This is not to say this process of negotiated obedience is always desirable, and it too may in fact be harmful, but it is indeed reality through certain stages of development. Rick Warren, as well as other conservative religious leaders, will fall back on his belief in absolute authority of scripture as reason for lack of compromise, his lack of tolerance for diversity of opinion or interpretation relative to traditional doctrine. Such a position is consistent with *his* set of life experiences -- family upbringing, cultural experience, study of literature, lessons learned as parent and pastor, and faith bolstered by his personal experience with God -- and he should be true to his beliefs. He should be commended for helping us to define purpose in our lives by bringing emphasis to the principles of leading a life reflecting God's love, serving and loving our neighbors, becoming more Christ-like in our daily lives, sharing in fellowship with our entire community, and in sharing the many invaluable teachings of the Bible. He delivers a very simple and effective message that hits home with many who come to the discussion equipped with cultural bias similar to his. But is it fair for Rick Warren or anyone else to answer the gamut of complex global religious questions with simple and singularly Christian answers? While it may be relatively simple for many Christians to use Christianity to define purpose and morality for certain aspects of their lives, don't confuse this with thinking that theological questions can be simply put in order by being obedient to culturally biased interpretation of God's mind and word.

Now here is the challenge, and the invitation, to the Rick Warrens of this world. We said Warren "should be true to his beliefs." How is it possible therefore to reconcile his beliefs with the "Christian Pluralist" philosophy outlined in Chapter I? Why should he want to? To do so requires being comfortable and secure in one's beliefs despite acknowledging doubts and inconsistencies exist. Many of us in the pews struggle with such thoughts during weekly sermons. But acknowledging contradictions in scripture does not have to relegate it to a thing of the past. Our invitation to our clergy is to stick with us as we offer insights into how a great many people consider these matters; the challenge is for all of us to keep an open mind as we contemplate answers to questions raised.

Recognize that the wisdom of a parent or religious leader is not without limits. There are other rational interpretations of scripture offered by reasonable people that provide insights into the complexity of the theological discussion. Those who choose to ignore or sidestep the complexity of religion, in order to deliver a simple message reassuring us that we don't have to critically think about doctrine presented, ultimately do us all a disservice. We will have taken a large step backward when we retreat into a world not embracing questioning. Religion has now grown out of its adolescence; as we have entered religious adulthood, it no longer suffices for any religious leader to say, "…because I tell you the scripture says it is so." It just isn't that simple. Lay people are not ignorant with respect to the complexities and inconsistencies dotting the landscape of the history of world religions. Don't "dumb down" the message for us. The advancement of human knowledge requires the challenging of traditional wisdom and the questioning of authority. To do so is as much a part of the human condition as is the inherent need to explore our spirituality. To deny this is to fly in the face of human experience.

Believing and *knowing* something however are two entirely different matters, though beliefs are often couched in terms reflecting a claim of absolute knowledge. Countless examples in history demonstrate the danger of absolute decrees born of limited knowledge or self-serving revelations. How many times have church leaders had to sheepishly apologize and retract erroneous statements of "fact" which for centuries survived unquestioned or with questions disallowed? Whether out of ignorance or greed, we make mistakes. Indeed parents, despite our most caring intentions, make mistakes. Should it be any surprise that leaders of world religions, products of the human condition, make mistakes and have been notorious for their well-meaning but misguided obstruction to inevitable change and progress? Can we not learn from mistakes of the past? Is it appropriate for us to be so sure of ourselves, so dogmatic, that we shun and exclude others who see life through a different lens? Is this compassion? Is this worshipping God?

In the following chapter we will explore further the notions of absolute authority and final revelations but for now can we consider where we may be in the evolution of religious thought and how our commitment to personal growth may extend to a commitment to religious evolution, acceptance, and diversity? Can we do so in a manner that allows us to be loyal to our traditions yet embracing of change and the emergence of new traditions for succeeding generations? Weren't our old traditions at one time new also? Is it possible for a God, active in our everyday lives, to reconcile the apparent paradox of accepting competing "truths" without being divisive and exclusionary? What kind of God is this? Does one definition of God fit all? Does our definition of God, our loyalty to the experiences we might share with God, require that we deny the experiences of our fellow believers? Is it time for us to give up control in the battle for theological enlightenment and supremacy?

Hollis, in The Middle Passage, speaks to the issue of parental control over their children: "The desire to control...to replicate our value system is not love; it is narcissism and it impedes their journey." As a community of religions should we strive for control, or dialogue? Control by parents provides comfort and security for children at an early age, but is parental control healthy when a son or daughter is no longer a child? Though it may be difficult to define, there comes a time when control must give way to trust, allowing the budding adult to make some mistakes even though as parents we still find ourselves trying to influence some choices. If we continue to demand obedience from our children once they have entered adulthood, then perhaps we have been unsuccessful in raising the independent, capable, and responsible contributor to society that should be the natural end product of parenting. We don't have to agree on everything, but shouldn't we be able to have dialogue, with mutual respect and love transcending our differences? Doesn't the teacher grow from the experience with the inquisitive, challenging pupil? Did not Jesus question the elders, challenge authority and traditional doctrine? Jesus embodied the inevitable evolution of religious thought. Jesus didn't emphasize doctrine, but rather delivered a simple message and exemplified a way of life -- ministering to others by putting aside self-centeredness, being all-inclusive, embracing those on the fringes of society, accepting diversity. Accepting the diversity of individuals and religions, and giving up control, invites us to make responsible new choices determining a new direction to our relationships. Successful relationships between individuals (and, we would suggest, between religions) require, according to Hollis: (1) Each partner must assume responsibility for their own psychological well being. (2) Commit to sharing their experience without reproaching the other for past wounds or future expectations. Listen to the other without being defensive. (3) Commit to sustain the dialogue. What would our world look like if leaders of "competing" religions adhered to these principles?

Those who have something to lose in the process, fearing past traditions and experiences are being demeaned or that their authority and control are being undermined, typically resist change. The comfort of knowing what the future might hold is lost. Such fears are unfounded, however, in the context of a healthy relationship as defined above. Successful relationships between religions do not require giving up the individuality of those same religions. As a global society, both religious and secular, we share common experiences now just as we have shared common origins, questions, conflicts, and spiritual quests. As theists, who have faith in an omnipresent God who entered into relationship with humankind through our conscious and subconscious selves well before the establishment of any formal religion or doctrine, are we not justified in believing that God's hand will continue to guide the evolution of religion *regardless* of formal doctrine? Even C.S. Lewis, recognized as one of the most influential Christian theologians of the twentieth century, though a staunch believer "that no man can be saved except through Christ," acknowledges in Mere Christianity that we should not be shackled by doctrine, stating that many people of other faiths (and should we extend this to atheists as well?) are attracted to Christ's example and "are being led by God's secret influence." He states his own belief in the "truth" of many traditional Christian concepts but at the same time advocates, "If any of them do not appeal to you, leave it alone and get on with the formula that does. And, whatever you do, do not start quarrelling with other people because they use a different formula than you." Though his beliefs -- those which provide comfort in interpreting past, present, and future -- work for him, does he not allow for change/evolution to be part of God's plan for others as he explains that Christians "offer an explanation of how God can be this impersonal mind at the back of the Moral Law and yet also a Person"?

This "impersonal mind" might be called our moral conscience by atheists, the "Ground of Being" by Bishop John Shelby Spong, or our basis for compassion by Buddha. Regardless of what we call this force, active within all of us and present well before any religious doctrine, which produces change, perhaps we should not fear it but rather embrace it. Wouldn't this be our greatest testimony to our faith in God's eternal nature and omnipresence? Do we trust in God's ability to transcend our changing moods, advances of science, new revelations and ongoing experiences? The discipline taught by the Torah, the love manifest by Jesus, the wisdom and teachings of Mohammed, the compassion embodied by Buddha are all tools placed at our disposal by some type of life force, regardless of whether we define or believe this force to be a personal God, an impersonal Spirit, or simply a moral conscience. Embracing change becomes much less threatening if believers have unlimited faith in their God coupled with the acceptance of the paradox that religious "truths" are not mutually exclusive. Christians, who have faith in matters beyond the ability of some to comprehend, such as the virgin birth of Jesus or the paradox of Jesus being both 100% human and 100% divine, should be able to lead others in the acceptance of conflicting "truths." Such acceptance must be heartfelt, not simply a tolerance of others' viewpoints; it must be beyond cordial and polite, all the while an undercurrent of distrust or superiority simmering unspoken; it must realize the validity of experiences and time unknown to any of us individually. John Dourley, Roman Catholic priest and Jungian analyst, states it beautifully in <u>The Illness That We Are: A Jungian Critique of Christianity</u> advocating that "diverse traditions would feel more at ease in seeing themselves as stones in a yet to be completed divine mosaic, each a partial but needed and valuable expression of the divine intent to become more fully conscious in history. Each could then more gladly look to others for aspects of the potential whole that in their own tradition are absent and perhaps all could look beyond themselves for a unity transcending their current sum total." Paradoxically then, to endorse the humble nature of each religion's place within the whole of our collective spirituality, it requires from the theist faith in a God active in a realm and manner beyond our ability to comprehend, but at the same time acknowledges and appreciates the experience and faith of traditional believers.

But how can a theist even begin to consider the idea of expanding one's concept of God? Doesn't this insult the experience of our forefathers and our own spiritual path? Can truth be relative without diminishing its value or significance for those who hold to such truths? Maybe this tolerant approach could have worked for Jews before God was revealed to them as documented through the Old Testament, or for Christians before God's "true" nature was manifest in the form of Jesus, or for Muslims before God's "final" revelations were spoken through Mohammed. But now the major monotheistic religions are in one sense trapped by their own dogma. Perhaps the key to unlocking the potential for harmonious relationships and mutual respect lies in rethinking the entire issue of absolute authority and final revelations, with a more deliberate focus on universal messages. Are we reaching a point in history where we can celebrate those facets of our faiths that unite us rather than fight over the differences which separate us? Pope John Paul II hosted in 1993 such a celebration with a concert at Vatican City for an audience of Catholics, Jews, Muslims, and representatives of Protestant and Orthodox churches. His message was one of healing relationships noting, "The history of relations among Jews, Christians, and Muslims is marked by light and darkness and unfortunately has known painful moments. Today one feels the pressing need for a sincere reconciliation among the believers in the one God. We are here together this evening to give concrete expression to this commitment to reconciliation, trusting in the universal message of music." Newly elected Pope Benedict XVI also has publicly given support to the ecumenical movement, but how can he do so while preaching the dangers of relativism and the need to not waver from traditional doctrine? Though bridging the chasm and celebrating universal themes has great appeal to most of us on some level, what holds us back from truly embracing our diversity? What is absolute authority? Can we, should we, share absolute authority? If shared, does that not make our "absolutes" relative?

DISCUSSION QUESTIONS

1) Does the analogy comparing individual with religious maturation make sense to me?

2) Do I think modern religions would more successfully develop healthy relationships with one another if they evolved away from some of the primitive images associated with their origins?

3) Have religions evolved over the past few thousand years, and will they do so in the future? What creates resistance to such evolution?

4) Is blind obedience to doctrine justifiable? What do I do if my reason and experience are in conflict with someone else's interpretation of God's will?

5) Is relativism a danger to organized religion?

CHAPTER IV

SACRED SCRIPTURES: LITERAL WORD OF GOD OR CHRONICLE OF THE SPIRITUAL JOURNEY?

America has the one true faith -- dozens of 'em.

Mark Twain

Andrew Sullivan in a *New York Times Review* (1/25/04) of The Trouble with Islam by Muslim reform activist Irshad Manji summarizes her convictions: "Her basic argument is that the Koran is a complex, contradictory, human book. Its proscriptions are many and conflicting. Abandoning the role of a thinking person is not something that should be required of any religious individual. Reason and faith, Manji wants to believe, are not in conflict. And yet, as Islam is frequently practiced, reason is deplored as something that must defer in every instance not simply to the Koran but to the political authoritarians who reserve to themselves the sole right to interpret it." How many Christians, horrified by the influence of Islamic fundamentalists, would applaud her insight and her efforts? Don't we believe absolutely that the world would be a better place if only Muslims could accept her well-reasoned concerns? What possibilities might abound if all Muslims endorsed open dialogue and freedom of dissent?

Westerners, unfamiliar with Islamic tradition, bitterly criticize the fundamentalists and the global divisiveness their views foment. Though we fail to understand what holds them back from accepting moderation and change, we still insist that *they* need to understand those factors impeding such progress. But is there more than just a little hypocrisy in our support of Manji's reform efforts? What prevents conservatives in any religion from embracing change? Is the Bible also a complex, contradictory, human book? What is the role of reason and experience in understanding and interpreting the Bible? Whose reason and experience is to be considered as ultimate authority? This is a most difficult subject with which to deal as we try to peel away thousands of years of tradition and competition amongst cultures and religions. Many traditionalists may share considerable agreement with us in theory to points raised thus far, but now we are getting down to the devil of the details. Now we will deal with specifics that may hit too close to home for some. To those individuals we would ask that you try to remember our bias. We recognize that it is our choice to not deny the fact that the concept of Christian Pluralism resonates with us. Our faith in pluralism we feel is a gift we wish to share with others. This is the perspective that requires us to confront contentious details. Only by doing so can we justify our own pluralist mentality and in turn invite the traditionalist to consider the same.

A dialogue:

T: I believe that the Bible represents God's plan for salvation. It spells out what I should do while here on earth and what my reward for following His plan will be. I believe the Bible was written by men and possibly women who were chosen by God to record His truth.

P: Do you believe that everything in the Bible is literally true?

T: That is a tough question. I know there are parts of the Bible, especially in the Hebrew Scripture, that are hard to understand. But we can't just start picking the parts we like and throwing away the parts that we think don't fit.

P: Why not? Some stories seem rather harsh and un-Godlike. God seems to change as the Bible progresses. His character and interaction with humans change dramatically from the stories in Genesis to later stories in Daniel, the Prophets and the New Testament. The theology also evolves and is not consistent. There seem to be contradictions and textual imperfections and inconsistencies that make it very hard to support the claim that the Bible is the literal "Word of God." Why do we have to cling to the parts that don't represent our understanding of God? What would be lost if we acknowledged that we no longer believe some of the stories represent an accurate portrait of God? Why can't we just say that that story worked for those people in that time, but it no longer works for us?

T: If we did that, the Bible would lose its authority. It would be just another storybook filled with ancient tales with no hold on us.

P: I don't think that is necessarily true. Sure, we would have to change our attitude toward the Bible's authority, but that doesn't mean we have to discard it as yesterday's news. The Bible is filled with wonderful insights into our search for God. It records the struggle our ancestors experienced trying to express their feelings about God and His character. I don't think continuing the struggle they began would cause us to leave God or the Bible behind. I believe it would free us to experience Him more completely. It is just like the search for truth in any mystery. There are going to be stories and descriptions and "truths" that work for a time and seem to explain the mystery, but later have to be left behind when new experiences and new knowledge render them unusable. Of course, we want to be scrupulous and very careful when deciding what is usable and what is not. We want to avoid the trap of saying a certain text is outdated when what we really mean is that it is too hard or demanding for us. There are going to be judgments about these subjects that are not going to please everyone. But that happens even now. Some denominations emphasize certain parts of the Bible and others emphasize others. That is why we have so many denominations. People see these things differently because they have different needs and come from different backgrounds.

For those grounded in a variety of traditions, believing that their scripture is *the* authoritative, final and only revelation from God brings a feeling of certainty rarely found in today's world. It is comforting to have one thing to believe that no new discovery or contradictory information can change. So many "truths" however once thought absolute have been tossed aside when new "truths" replace them. Think of those who believed absolutely that the Earth was the center of the universe or that the world was flat or that the heavens were a dome above the Earth. The list goes on and on, with science replacing old facts with the new. The information age demands new ways of approaching old problems. But biblical truths are seen in a different light, are accepted as given from an authority not to be questioned, and with this acceptance comes some degree of comfort. That comfort has a high price, however. It means we have to hang on to images of God even when they no longer seem to fit. It means we have to exclude children from God's kingdom because they don't believe the same things we do. For some, this price is becoming too high to pay. We must find a way to move beyond some of the passages that hold us back as people of God, trying to embrace all as brothers and sisters, no matter what their beliefs or customs.

People of faith harbor strong opinions about their sacred texts. As such, any discussion of these texts is bound to summon quick and, sometimes, emotional responses. We understand the reader will be offended by our stating a few controversial and unpopular ideas concerning the sacred text of the Christian and Jewish faith, but we believe understanding the Bible (or the sacred scripture of any religion) in a non-traditional way holds the key to people of all faiths coming together as brothers and sisters on the same journey --seeking God. Many of the ideas stated here are not new or original. Other writers have said the same things in more eloquent ways. We add our voices to continue the dialogue, to encourage respectful exchanges between peoples of all faiths, and even among those who claim no faith. To genuinely come together for this journey, we must face the issues of Biblical authority and the claim by some religions that theirs is the true and final revelation from God. This does not mean we need to discard the Bible or other sacred texts or re-write them or deny their marvelous contributions to human progress and the search for God. We simply want to propose a way to embrace the scriptures without being limited by them, for we feel insistence on strict, literal adherence to any scripture is an obstacle to our becoming people of God.

We feel that a large number of people yearn to reach out to fellow seekers of other faiths to embrace them and affirm their journey. But they hesitate because they feel they are betraying the principles of their own faith as recorded in the sacred scriptures. We strive through the ensuing discussion to encourage them and provide a few methods for grappling with this potentially divisive subject matter. If one can reach the goal of embracing other faiths by other means, then this discussion is perhaps unnecessary. But if the reader struggles with this issue, then read on and be encouraged.

We owe a great debt to the authors of the sacred texts of all faiths. These works form the heart of our search for a better life for all people and our search for God, by whatever name God is known. Huston Smith wrote in the forward to Philip Novak's <u>The</u>

World's Wisdom, "Whether revelation issues from God or from the deepest unconscious of spiritual geniuses can be debated, but its signature is invariably power... People respond to this news of life's larger meaning because they hear in it the final warrant for their existence." Smith's point is that reading and studying sacred scriptures adds meaning to their lives. In fact, these texts transform lives. People are moved by these texts to be more than they would be without them. Reading them inspires humanity to care for the least and the lost, to throw off selfishness in favor of caring and to build societies where justice can prevail. This is a great endeavor and one from which the world has benefited greatly, but there are passages in many of the sacred texts that continue to divide us and make us competitors rather than brothers and sisters.

We will discuss the Christian Bible that contains the Hebrew scripture. Others will have to look at the sacred scriptures of their own faith, but we hope they will come to similar conclusions. If not, then perhaps at least we can respect the right of each of us to search for God in our own way. In our search as we try to reconcile apparent contradictions and inconsistencies within the Bible, we must first ask, "What is the Bible and how did it become the Bible?" The Bible is a complex and often impenetrable collection of stories, poetry, songs, and history compiled over centuries by a variety of scribes and editors. Even making that statement is bound to elicit negative responses by some who believe that God is the author of the Bible and human secretaries only provided the quill and papyrus. Others believe God inspired the authors but did not dictate the text. Even the word "inspire" is given different meanings depending on the perspective of the person defining the word. Christian denominations debate these issues at conferences and in Sunday school classes all over the world. People even leave their congregations due to disagreements over how the Bible was written and what authority it has over the faith.

Emerson Colaw, in his book <u>Beliefs of a United Methodist Christian</u>, writes, "We believe that the Bible is a result of the efforts of both the Holy Spirit and ordinary persons.... In all this we are simply trying to say that the Bible is a very human book in its origins and translations, and has profoundly influenced our human institutions in western civilization. But it also contains the inspired Word of God...the principle of inspiration was accepted, but uniformity of inspiration was not...it is not magical nor is it faultless." All these statements point to the conclusion that the Bible contains a mixture of divine and human. This combination can make the study and understanding of the Bible very difficult. People are bound to read passages and disagree over the meaning and universality of them. Some United Methodists will even disagree with Colaw's words describing United Methodists' beliefs about the Bible.

For the past century or so, scholars have written hundreds of books attempting to shed light on the questions of authorship, sources, influences, historical context, questions of language and translation, and the original meaning of the authors and editors. Biographies and histories of God are now available, written by brilliant and learned scholars. Commentaries on each book of the Bible abound. Study Bibles provide footnotes and references trying to explain arcane references that baffle the casual reader. Archeologists publish books concerning new interpretations of old evidence and the meaning of new evidence found in the ongoing search for the "truth" of the Bible. Discoveries at Qumran and Nag Hammadi of the Dead Sea Scrolls and the Gnostic writings answered some questions but also raised many more. We struggle over what the Bible says and how it is presented. There are conflicting claims made by commentaries; theologians argue over the authenticity of certain texts; seminars proclaim what Jesus really said as opposed to what was added later by the authors. All of this is very confusing and disconcerting to the faithful student of Christianity. From the pulpit we hear of the "truth" contained in the Bible, but the scholarship seems to say otherwise. We search for a way to engage the Bible without having to accept it as the authoritative and only "Word of God."

It is possible some of the details of the stories in the Bible are not historically, or even theologically, accurate, but they do contain essential truths for people of faith. God's involvement is the key element supporters of the inerrant Bible point to as the source of the Bible's authority. They believe that if the Bible is the Word of God, then it cannot contain any mistakes or inaccuracies. The extent of God's involvement is also the one element that cannot be defined or studied or agreed upon. There is no way to prove the extent to which God was involved in the formation of the Bible. It is impossible to quantify God's involvement in any endeavor. There is no way to measure or trace or discover the presence of God in the texts of the Bible by studying or analyzing it. We accept God's presence on faith. The belief that God inspired or authored the Bible is one of the key tenets of Christian and Jewish faith. Most churches or denominations include such a belief in their written doctrines. It is preached from the pulpits and taught to the young and our converts. But efforts to prove scientifically that God authored or inspired the Bible are futile.

Men and women continue to claim to receive communications and revelations from God. However, they are not given the status or belief that they were in ancient times. No writings or teachings or proclamations today carry the mantle of "Word of God." One reason for this is the tendency to attribute more authority and purity to times of the distant past than to the present. We often look to a past time as a "Golden Age" when everything was better and purer and superior. In his book <u>From the Maccabees to the Mishnah</u>, Shaye J.D. Cohen says, "Jewish literature of the second temple period was the product of two contradictory tendencies. On the one hand, the Jews sensed they were living in a postclassical age and that it was their duty to collect, venerate, and study the works of their great ancestors. *This tendency yielded the Bible* and the idea that classical prophecy is no longer alive." [Italics added.] In other words, at some point in time, people decided that stories from long ago represented a better, truer and divinely inspired reality that could not be replicated in the present sinful age. They felt their ancestors were closer to God and more in tune with God than they were. God's favor was bestowed upon them by communicating directly with them, whereas this no longer occurs because of the fallen nature of the present world. Therefore, the stories of those ancient times needed to be set apart and studied and revered more so than anything produced by contemporary sages.

The people of the Second Temple Period, about 520 BCE (Before Common Era) until about the first century CE, had just been through a national crisis and a crisis of faith. All their stories of God led them to believe they were under divine protection and that they would be delivered from the hands of their enemies. The stories they had heard throughout their lives told of God's promise to make of them a great nation and that they were the chosen people. Their mighty *Yahweh* could not possibly be defeated by the evil Babylonian god. It just didn't fit. God was in charge of the universe and yet chosen ones were carried off into captivity by worshippers of another god. The only true God could not be humiliated. There had to be another way to explain this event. The explanation that came to be accepted was that God was the author of their defeat. God did not suffer the defeat and humiliation; the people did. This catastrophe happened because of their sinfulness. They deserved to be punished, and God used Nebuchadnezzar to punish their evil ways. This led to the process of collecting and venerating the texts from the past and making the Hebrew Scriptures. Cohen said, "Now ... all these books were closed [even if their texts remained fluid for some time]. Not only were the words of anonymous seers no longer added to those of the named prophets, but no one any longer saw heavenly visions and heard heavenly voices quite like those of previous times. Prophecy continued, but its method and message were different from those of Isaiah, Jeremiah and Ezekiel and their authors now hid behind pseudonyms or false identities (a practice know as 'pseudepigraphy')."

For centuries, prior to this period, the texts we know as Biblical went through the process of being told, re-told, re-worded and written according to changing times and circumstances. Editors added and deleted based on new information or changing theology. Now this process came to a close. No longer were people deemed worthy to update the sacred texts. These various rabbis, scribes and priests decided which texts were deemed worthy and which were not. Some of the ones deemed not worthy were still read and revered, but were considered less authoritative. The designation applied to them was "Apocrypha." How they decided the worthiness of the texts is not fully known. Many believers say God decided, but of course, we can't know for sure. We can, however, study the texts and draw some conclusions that may help us determine what place the Bible should have in our faith journey.

Jack Miles, in his book <u>God, A Biography</u>, tries to illustrate that God as a character in the Bible developed as time went by. He followed the development of God's many personalities and described the sequence in the Hebrew Bible as going from "Action to Speech to Silence." God's personality changed as the people's understanding of God changed. Reading the Bible sometimes causes great confusion about which characterization of God is the dominant or true one. Miles further states, "There is much to object to in Him, and many attempts have been made to improve Him. Much that the Bible says about Him is rarely preached from the pulpit because, examined too closely, it becomes a scandal. But if only some of the Bible is actively preached, none of the Bible is quite denied." In Hebrew Scriptures we read about the warrior God who is very much concerned with conquering and disposing of enemies. Some of the stories portray God as harsh and quite willing to cause the death and destruction of His creation. The story of the flood and Noah is a particularly gruesome example. Sunday School students all over the world draw rainbows and doves and sing songs about the animals in the ark, but reading the text gives a very different picture. In Genesis 6:6 the author says, "And the Lord was sorry that he had made humankind on the earth, and it grieved him to his heart. So, the Lord said, "I will blot out from the earth the human beings I have created -- people together with animals and creeping things and birds of the air, for I am sorry that I have made them." There are many puzzling points in this passage. Where are the concepts of grace and forgiveness and love that give us such comfort as we hear them preached from the pulpit? It is unlikely that those people in antiquity were much different from us. The twentieth century certainly ranks as one of the most violent in world history, and yet we were not condemned to die in a horrible flood. The animals certainly didn't perpetrate evil, and yet they were killed along with the people. To many readers, this story does not reflect an accurate image of the God they worship. Yet we continue to tell the story and try to find a positive spin for it, so we concentrate on the rainbow.

Another conundrum contained in the story is how an omniscient and omnipotent God can be sorry for anything. An all-knowing, all-seeing God certainly knew humankind would sin once created. If God created us and gave us free will, then certain consequences would be expected to follow. The regret attributed to God in this passage seems to be a vestige of an ancient version of God that is no longer credible. We certainly don't talk about God regretting actions in today's world. Commentaries on the text point to the similarities between the Biblical account and the Babylonian Gilgamesh Epic and say that the Bible story added a purpose for the flood as opposed to the Gilgamesh portrayal of "polytheistic caprice." The Genesis interpretation of an old story then attempts to bring a well-accepted story into the language of God, but it doesn't quite work. The people of that age seem to have projected onto God their own human traits of anger and regret and punishment.

A dialogue:

P: The story of the flood in Genesis 6 recounts images of God that no longer mesh with the God to whom we pray or worship. In this story God says He is sorry for having created humankind. They were wicked and He decided to blot out all living creatures (even the innocent animals) except the family of Noah and a pair of each animal species. This seems very harsh. We see evil all around us today. The twentieth century surely has to be one of the most violent and evil in human history, but God did not blot us out. Why then and not now? The Interpreter's Bible says this story was almost certainly borrowed from an ancient Babylonian myth contained in the Gilgamesh Epic. If this is true, what are the implications? Why did the writers of Genesis include it?

T: God led them to include it. That is what "Word of God" means.

P: But why? What was God trying tell us? That he will kill us if we cross Him? Apparently not, since we have crossed Him many times, even before Christ died to offer forgiveness for our sins. Furthermore, the emotions attributed to God don't seem very Godlike. They seem very human. How can God be sorry He created humankind? If He is God, should not He have known His creation would become violent and less than perfect? How can this story be an accurate portrayal of the God we worship? He killed women and children and babies. Is that befitting a God who in other passages tells us to take care of the orphan and the widow? Does it fit?

T: You are forgetting the rainbow and God's promise.

P: You're right. That is an integral part of the story. God promises never to destroy the earth again by means of a flood. He says, "I will never again curse the ground because of man, for the imagination of man's heart is evil from his youth; neither will I ever again destroy every living creature as I have done." Does this mean He made a mistake? Is He repenting? Did He just now realize the true nature of man, that his "heart is evil from his youth?" All these questions point to the fact that this story describes a God very human in His behavior and thinking. Is this the God we worship?

T: You are emphasizing those points that support your argument. I think the story illustrates God's willingness to give everyone a second chance. He wants us to walk with Him and follow Him.

P: Don't we all read the Bible through tinted glasses? Don't we all pick and choose those verses we feel comfortable with? You can't deny that the verses I use are there. I can't deny the rainbow is there. Our experience and our needs dictate how we process the story.

In Exodus, in the story of Moses and the Pharaoh, God is described as "hardening" the heart of the Pharaoh so he would not let the Israelites leave. "Go to the Pharaoh; for I have hardened his heart and the heart of his officials, in order that I may show these signs of mine among them, and that you may tell your children and grandchildren how I have made fools of the Egyptians and what signs I have done among them -- so that you may know that I am the Lord" (Exodus 10:1-2). This motif is repeated over and over again throughout the story, so the message is clear. God caused the Egyptians to refuse to let the people go so God could perpetrate the plagues, even the last plague which killed every first born of the land -- even the animals. God did this to show God's unchallengeable might and power to the Israelites and the Egyptians. This behavior does not reflect our current image of God. Certainly it is not the image being advertised or talked about very much. More likely this portrait of God causes a great number of believers to squirm in their pews when they think about it or read it in their Bibles. Modern interpreters try to explain God's actions by saying God would not harden a heart that was not already hardened, but this is not what the text says. It says unequivocally that God hardened Pharaoh's heart for a very specific reason.

There are innumerable other references that cause many readers to balk and conclude that the Bible contains images and passages that no longer apply to our faith journey. The books of Joshua and Judges tell of God ordering the Israelites to kill all inhabitants of cities. In Joshua 8:1ff, "The Lord said to Joshua, 'Do not fear or be dismayed: take all the fighting men with you, and go up now to Ai.

72

See, I have handed over to you the King Ai with his people, his city, and his land. You shall do to Ai and its king as you did to Jericho and its king; only its spoil and its livestock you may take as booty for yourselves.'" In Joshua 6:17 the author tells us Joshua destroyed all the inhabitants of Jericho, except Rahab and her house. Here God is ordering mass murder, and this is not an isolated incident. It happens over and over that God induces followers to brutalize their enemies. We try to deal with this brutality attributed to God in very creative ways. We want so badly to find a way to make this image of God conform to one with which we can be comfortable that we invent all sorts of rationalizations. In the end, though, we may just have to admit that the God described here is not the God we worship. Even within the canonical books God's behavior and attitude change. We see a very different God described in Daniel than the one in Joshua. What are we to make of this evolution of thought? It is unlikely that the authors were trying to deceive the readers, nor did they harbor barbarous notions of who God was. They simply lived in a different time and place, and their vision of God helped them understand what was happening to them, in the context of their own set of life experiences, consistent with the lens through which they viewed life's struggles. Gods in those cultures fought wars beside their believers. The people with the stronger god won. They believed, as most in their day did, that the divine beings controlled and orchestrated all aspects of life. They ascribed to God the positive and negative, both the fortunate and the unfortunate, and then they tried to explain why God did things that seemed cruel or destructive. They tried to fathom the unfathomable by describing the reason God caused harmful or cruel events.

In the early stages of Biblical theology, no Evil One existed. God was the source of all. Only later did the concept of a devil or Evil One or Satan become part of the religious landscape. Gradually, the Devil became the one responsible for the evil and cruelty; this left God as the author of good and righteous acts. Elaine Pagels, in her book The Origin of Satan, says that the concept of Satan as known to us from Western Christianity was largely absent from the Hebrew Scriptures. The word *Satan* appears in Numbers, Job and a few other places in the Hebrew Scriptures, but the character it names is not the Evil One of New Testament literature. Our notion of who God was (and is) evolved over time and required new answers to old questions. No longer could believers accept a God that caused death and destruction indiscriminately. Another explanation had to be found for all the negative and incomprehensibly foul acts, and the Devil or Satan filled the need. Jeffrey Burton Russell wrote in The Devil, Perceptions of Evil from Antiquity to Primitive Christianity:

> No longer easy in their minds about ascribing rapine and destruction to the will of their God, the Hebrews sought new theodicies. One was that evil was the result of the sin of humanity....[but] the corrupt will of human beings seemed insufficient to explain the vast and terrifying quantity of evil in the world.

> For an answer, the Hebrews turned to another explanation: the instigator of evil was a malignant spirit whose power to offend was far greater than that of mortals.

They discarded a theory of God and God's nature that no longer worked for them. Changing sensibilities and new experiences required new answers.

This same evolutionary process also applies to the concept of an afterlife (heaven and hell) as eternal reward or punishment. It is clear from the Hebrew Scriptures that the afterlife, if they believed in it at all, did not involve reward or punishment. It was the shadowy Sheol (the "pit" for souls after death, regardless of their character while alive). The ancient Hebrews believed God punished or rewarded people for their deeds in their earthly life. If you became sick or suffered misfortune, you must have sinned. If you prospered, it was God's doing as a reward for your righteousness. Most Christians no longer accept this theology because they see evidence all around them that the formula doesn't work. Bad things do indeed happen to good people. Another theology of reward and punishment must be found. Even in Jesus' time some Jews (Sadducees) still did not accept an afterlife or resurrection after death. They still believed that earthly life was all there was. This uneven theology seems to further erode the claim that the Bible is "true" in all its images and stories and pronouncements.

A close look at some of the New Testament writings also raises questions about the claim of inerrancy and absolute authority of the Bible. In the Gospels of Matthew and Luke genealogies are provided to illustrate Jesus' direct lineage from David, a prerequisite for the Messiah. The problem is that they do not agree with one another. Interpreters again try to explain the discrepancies away, but no matter what the explanation it seems one of the two must be in factual error. Another difference is that both Matthew and Luke describe Jesus as being born of a virgin and both trace his lineage through Mary's husband Joseph. Both claims of virgin birth and direct lineage from King David through Joseph cannot be accurate. They are mutually exclusive.

Furthermore, other aspects of the Gospel narrative's account of Jesus' birth and life bother the historian E.P. Sanders. He says that the story in Matthew 2:16 probably did not occur. He writes, "Herod was ruthless and he did kill people who seemed to pose a threat to his reign, including [as we saw above] his favorite wife and their two sons plus one of his sons by another wife. Did he slaughter 'all the male children in Bethlehem and in all that region who were two years old or under?' It is not likely. Josephus narrated a lot of stories about Herod, dwelling on his brutality, but not this one." If, as Sanders says, the event didn't happen, why did Matthew write it? It is suggested that he wrote it for the same reason he wrote many other stories about Jesus -- to make his point that Jesus was the fulfillment of certain scriptures contained in the Hebrew Scriptures. Matthew or the writer of Matthew believed this, and he wanted to persuade his readers to believe it. There are many other examples of this phenomenon in the Gospels. These were not dishonest men trying to perpetrate fraud. They believed in Jesus and used their knowledge of scripture to make their case. They too had their biases stemming from their own experiences: traditions, oral histories passed on from one generation to the next, teachings from revered present-day scholars, their own direct observations, and ultimately their own faith. Actual events did not concern them in the same manner we expect of historical documents today. Their contribution of timeless value was that they wrote theology, but they did not attempt to write history, as we know it. Problems occur when people today want to read it as both history and theology and apply today's standards of scholarship and understanding. But this should not take away from acknowledging the fact that the discussion burns on 2000 years later. One might reasonably argue that this fact alone speaks to the likelihood that they were chronicling a series of events surrounding the life of Jesus that were indeed exceptional, consistent with divine influence, and fully deserving of their place in history, even if all the "facts" do not necessarily add up.

To be sure, certain parts of both the Hebrew Scripture and the New Testament are historically accurate. The people of Judea were carried off into captivity by the Babylonians. They did return to Judea and live there once again. King Herod really existed. Pontius Pilate ruled over Jerusalem. The Romans did execute many people. No one doubts that Jesus lived and taught in Palestine in more or less the time described in the Gospels. Jesus taught and lived and died. Beyond these "facts" we cannot *know* much else for certain. Now we must have a definition of terms here, lest this seem too harsh and dismissive. We consider the word *know* to imply incontrovertible fact, that which can be agreed upon by historical and scientific experts studying a particular event. Recognize however that there is a different type of knowledge applicable to matters of the spiritual realm. Equally valid, this is experiential and faith-based and for the possessor of such a perspective it is every bit as real as scientific fact. It is no more defensible for those of us who do not share this experience to dismiss such feelings as mere rationalizations than it is for the traditional believer to try to defend doctrine using academic "factual" arguments, as both of these positions result in divisiveness with little chance of resolution. But we still can learn from Jesus, regardless of whether one believes in His divinity. His words as recorded in the New Testament shine through with timeless truths. It is good and it has always been good to feed the hungry, clothe the naked, and free the oppressed. Humility, kindness to strangers, help to the poor, and loving one's neighbors can never be wrong. We feel it in our hearts and souls. It resonates. The problem is that some of the sayings and writings cause division and enmity among God's children, and yet we are told they must be true because they are in the Bible. We are told we must believe and follow them because to do otherwise would be to renounce God and Jesus. But we have tried through several examples to illustrate the problems with the claims that the Bible is the authoritative, inerrant word of God. We know this issue could be debated endlessly and reasonable people can disagree about the validity of the arguments presented here. We posit, however, that reasonable people cannot *know* which argument is correct. We cannot absolutely *know* the mind of God. Many of us have strong beliefs and feelings anchored in a foundation of life's experiences unique to each of us as individuals. But, because we cannot *know*, we further propose that we cannot close the book on the discussion. Perhaps establishing the canon was not the wisest choice, in the long run. We mentioned previously the words of the author Shaye J.D. Cohen about the reasons the Hebrew Scriptures were closed to further revelations. Certainly there is a need to have some organization and closure to generations of discussion, but in light of current knowledge and experience and reason, it may be time to revisit the idea. There is a possibility that God's purposes might be served by expanding our sacred canon.

The same canonical process occurred for New Testament texts. Over time and with great debate church councils and church officials decided on twenty-seven books from the dozens available that were deemd authorative enough to be part of the New Testament. Those who used other texts that were considered against church teachings were treated as outcasts or worse. We all know the stories of the Inquisitions and other efforts by the church to enforce "right thinking". Many times throughout the centuries orthodox leaders denounced the "heretics" by saying they were serving Satan. Only official, orthodox views were allowed to exist within the church body. Of course, over the years, interpretation of these texts has changed dramatically, but we still have only those twenty-seven books to interpret and debate.

The first question that cries to be asked is, "By what authority did the rabbis, priests and church officials make the decision to stop the process of divine revelation?" Authority in the early Christian church derived from a real or perceived link to the early apostles who knew Jesus personally. As we know, Jesus did not author any letters or statements of doctrine Himself. So the apostles were the closest we can get to firsthand accounts. Many writings were published using the names of different apostles to give them the weight of that connection. The quickest way to dispose of a theology as wrong or as heresy was to show how the apostles did not endorse it. That is why authorship of the texts is so hard to determine. Using someone else's name as the author of a particular letter or tract was not considered illegal or immoral. The gospels Matthew, Mark, Luke and John were attributed to well-known figures whose names carried authority. Whether those same people wrote them is widely debated. Most scholars believe they were not. The New Oxford Annotated Bible states in the introduction to the Gospel of Matthew, "This Gospel is anonymous. The unknown Christian teacher who prepared it during the last third of the first century may have used as one of his sources a collection of Jesus' sayings that the apostle Matthew, according to second-century writers, is said to have drawn up. In time a title containing Matthew's name, and signifying apostolic authority, came to identify the whole." Similar statements appear in the introductions of the other three Gospels. These authors did not write for fame or notoriety; they wrote to teach and persuade. They needed credibility and using the name of an apostle with a direct connection to Jesus gave them that. We should not accept this connection uncritically, and the authority it implies, as the only true and final revelation. When examining the motivations and circumstances surrounding the formation of the canon, we see some of the assertions and statements as less than authoritative.

Committees, councils and individuals participated in the process of canonization of both Hebrew and Christian scripture. Their reasons, no doubt, seemed very sound and justifiable to them. In the case of the Christian texts, the church officials of the third and fourth centuries CE wanted to define the correct or "orthodox" theology concerning Jesus and His nature. Diversity seemed to threaten the movement still in its infancy. The church leaders wanted to exclude all those writings and teachings that did not conform to their beliefs. Why the need to agree on the nature of Jesus and its theology? The Emperor Constantine and other church officials felt a unified church that recognized their authority could enhance their power and authority. They also felt the very life of the church was at stake. Elaine Pagels writes in <u>Beyond Belief, The Secret Gospel of Thomas</u>:

> To strengthen his own alliance with church leaders and to unify fractious Christian groups into one harmonious structure, Constantine charged bishops from churches throughout the empire to meet at his expense at Nicea, an inland city near a large lake, to work out a standard formulation of Christian faith. From that meeting and its aftermath, during the tumultuous decades that followed, emerged the Nicene Creed that would effectively clarify and elaborate the "canon of truth" along with what we call the canon -- the list of twenty-seven writings which would become the New Testament. Together these would help establish what Irenaeus had envisioned -- a worldwide communion of "orthodox" Christians joined into one "catholic and apostolic" church.

Constantine knew it would be easier to rule over a homogenous group of believers than over a fractious one. That doesn't mean that all the participants in the Council of Nicea were as cynical as Constantine. They held their beliefs fervently and passionately and debates raged over what to include in the official version of the "New Testament." The point here is not to question their sincerity, but their authority. Did they have the right to effectively shut down the debate and end the search for the meaning of Jesus' life and ministry? Even after the Council issued its decisions, many ignored them and continued to worship and write and teach according to their own beliefs, but it became increasingly difficult for them. Persecutions and even executions began to take place for those who did not conform. The orthodox bishops had the power and might of Constantine and the Roman Empire, but whether they possessed special authority from God is open to question. Again, no one knows for sure, and, as we all know, winners write the histories. The writings of the rival theologies were systematically sought out and destroyed so we know very little of their total structure and substance. Fortunately, some of the manuscripts were saved and discovered at Nag Hammadi in 1945, but we still don't have a clear picture of the different beliefs held during this very difficult time. We can never know for certain if God directed the making of the canon or to what extent God inspired the writing of it. We can only study the texts and try to draw our own conclusions. Most Christians who enter Bible study do so from the perspective that it is the Word of God and cannot be "wrong" or "untrue" or contain inaccuracies concerning God. This attitude, of course, colors how the texts are understood and interpreted. We believe we must put aside that bias for a time to really assess the scriptures objectively.

That brings us to another question: "Was it a good idea to form the Biblical canon?" There is no clear and unequivocal answer. There are obvious advantages, administratively, for everyone studying and learning the same texts, especially if those texts endorse one's claim of authority. The church body accepts the opinions of the bishops and priests, and for the most part, they don't question their interpretations of the Holy Scripture. Practical matters such as finances or mass communication can be handled with greater efficiency and purpose. A large body of like-minded people can accomplish a great deal if they are led with vision and purpose. Great good can be done by a huge organization dedicated to bringing about the Kingdom of God on Earth. Debate over theology is held to a minimum. All these things make it easier to grow and expand the church to do God's work.

However, there are downsides to the canon. Just as great good can be done in the name of God by a large, cohesive organization, great harm can also be done. Dissension and disagreement can be squelched easily, and minority opinions can be silenced ruthlessly. The majority can even demonize people who choose a different path. We only have to look at the Crusades and the Inquisition to find examples of this practice. Also, stifling the search for the meaning and nature of Jesus deprives us of a great gift of the spiritual journey. We have to rein in our spiritual yearnings to conform to church teachings. We can't experience Jesus in ways that do not meet with church approval. Sadly, the idea that one size fits all in theology is probably a bad idea. We can see this even within the church body. The proliferation of denominations and sects within Christianity illustrates the great yearning for a theology that speaks personally to the believer. Think of all the spiritual power and creativity lost by confining the dialogue to just the canonized scripture. The soul can soar when allowed to do so. It is perfectly natural for humanity to see the divine in different forms. We all have different realities and experiences. We see the world from eyes formed by those experiences and to demand that we all feel God's presence in the same manner is, at best, naïve, and, at worst, tyrannical.

Furthermore, changing times and historical trends call for adjustments in thinking and sensitivities. A casual glance at the laws in Exodus, Leviticus, Numbers and Deuteronomy illustrates the point. In Exodus 21 there are rules for buying and selling slaves and rules for selling one's own daughter. They do not say, "Don't sell your daughter," but rather they say that if you do, she will not be treated as male slaves are. Death penalties abound. Verse 15 says whoever strikes father or mother shall be put to death. Verse 17 says whoever curses his father or mother shall be put to death. And on and on. In the New Testament Paul writes to the churches in Asia Minor about rules for behavior for both men and women. He writes of proper dress and proper ways to adorn one's self. In his letter to Timothy, he instructs women to dress modestly, with no braided hair or gold. He wrote to the church at Corinth in 1 Corinthians 7 that if sex can be avoided, it should be, but it is better to marry than to let the passion eat away at you. In letters to the Ephesians, Colossians, and Timothy, Paul implicitly condones the practice of slavery. The writers of the Gospels of John and Luke felt the world, as we know it, would not last very much longer. They felt the end of the age was near. (John 21:22) (Luke 9:27). Jesus told His disciples that some would live to see the kingdom of God established on Earth. Most of us ignore Paul's proscriptions about dress and sex and are offended by the practice of slavery in any form. The majority also no longer believes that the end of the world, as it might relate to the Second Coming, is imminent.

Most readers and interpreters of these passages water them down or dismiss them outright by pointing to the historical context and the fact that times and attitudes have changed. This is reasonable, but the implications for the rest of the Bible are profound. Who gets to decide what matters and what doesn't? Who gets to decide what passages are taken literally and what passages are to be interpreted as metaphor or allegory or put in historical context as not relevant to our world? If we are able to ignore certain parts of the Bible but insist on strict adherence to others because it is the word of God, aren't we contradicting ourselves? Homosexuality is one example where many church leaders insist on strict adherence to the Biblical text. In Leviticus "lying with a man as a woman" is called an abomination, but lying with a woman during her menses is also called condemned in the same chapter. Why is one true for all times and the other only true in ancient times? If we believe word of mouth and studies by various sex researchers, a good percentage of people practice a condemned act by ancient standards and no one flinches, but homosexuality causes churches to split and members to leave in anger. Some may scoff at Old Testament inconsistencies and point to the New Testament wherein Jesus makes reference to marriage being between a man and a woman. But recall that Jesus also gave credence to the concept of slavery and spoke of the characteristics of a good slave versus a poor one. This we certainly would not consider to be a politically correct line of discussion today. Why do some ignore the slavery comments and focus on marriage and sexuality issues? Could it be that some of the "errors" in Jesus' ways reflect the aforementioned concept that Jesus may be human and divine at the same time? Could it be that some social commentary was simply his human reflection of the prevailing culture of the times, whereas other messages carried a divine character contributing to their timeless application to our lives still today?

Furthermore, Christians largely ignore one of the Ten Commandments and not much is said. Exodus 20:8 says, "Remember the Sabbath day, and keep it holy. Six days you shall labor and do all your work. But the seventh day is a Sabbath to the Lord your God; you shall not do any work -- you, your son or your daughter, your male or female slave, your livestock, or the alien resident in your towns. For in six days the Lord made heaven and earth, the sea and all that is in them, but rested the seventh day; therefore the Lord blessed the Sabbath day and consecrated it." We eat in restaurants, go to malls, mow our grass, play golf, go to movies, football games...on Sundays and we work 24 hours/day, 7 days/week, 365 days/year; yet we don't hear admonitions from pulpits saying we are jeopardizing our eternal lives by not staying home and meditating on God. Somehow modern Christians have decided this commandment no longer applies to them.

In Matthew 12:1 Jesus is accused of breaking the Sabbath by picking corn and feeding His disciples. In answering the charge He does not say, "The Sabbath no longer applies," or "My followers do not have to keep the Sabbath because I am making new rules." He acknowledges the importance of the Sabbath but says it can be modified in certain instances. Obviously, Jesus respected the

Sabbath and kept it, unless a life was placed in jeopardy by strictly following the letter of the law instead of the spirit of the law. We live in a world that has no down time, and it is not convenient to set aside a day for God and rest. Our world never closes. We justify ignoring the Sabbath by saying the world has changed. No longer do we have the luxury of a "day of rest."

Throughout the New Testament Jesus tells His followers to live simply, to give to the poor, to share wealth. He even tells people to give away all they have and follow Him. (See Luke 9:3-5; 57-62, Luke 12:22-34, Luke 16:19-31, and on and on.) We deal with these passages in a similar fashion. We interpret them to mean something other than what they say. We say they mean, "Don't let money or wealth stand between you and God." Or, "Have compassion for the poor." Or, "Have your priorities straight, put God first." We say God didn't really mean we were supposed to give away *everything*. God would not want us to all to be poor. It wouldn't make sense if all people gave away all their wealth. In other words, we interpret these difficult passages using our reason and experience. We don't take the Bible literally. We mention it here to illustrate that Christians have a history of adapting to changing times, even if it means not precisely following all the verses in the Bible. This is not a new concept.

The larger question for us, then, is can we leave behind those passages that no longer work or are no longer in sync with our experience of the nature of God? By doing this are we betraying the faith? We don't think so. We are just continuing the process started in ancient times, but temporarily halted by the church fathers when they formed the canon. If God did not reveal all to the early writers of the Hebrew Scriptures (e.g. Satan, heaven and hell), perhaps there is more to be revealed to us. The early images of God as the Warrior God were not the end of the story. The ancient sages continued to search for meaning and for God after they occupied the Promised Land and were defeated by the Babylonians. They did not abandon God when their needs were no longer met, but they did change their ideas about who God was and the nature of their interactions. Continuing to search for God allows us to expand God's message to include more and more people.

Even if the reader is not convinced by the preceding discussion concerning the nature of the Bible and its authority, there are other methods of reading the Bible, as it is written, that allow acceptance of other faiths as equal partners in the quest for God. Interpretation of the Bible and its ancient images has gone on since the very beginning. Discussion about God's interaction with humanity began when the first story was told around the first campfire in those ancient times when our thoughtful, brilliant ancestors started this journey to know and understand God's ways. James L. Kugel, in his book The Bible as It Was, said, "For, even before the Bible had attained its final form, its stories, songs and prophecies had begun to be *interpreted* [Author's italics]." We interpret the Bible every time we sit down to read it. We do this subconsciously and constantly. We could even say all reading involves interpretation in some manner. We form opinions and make connections from our knowledge and experience and form mental images of the characters and places contained in the text as we read, and these become the truth for us.

We do this with all the books we read, not just the Bible. We do it when we see movies, when we hear the evening news, and when we tell stories about our past to our children. At Thanksgiving dinner tables around the country parents tell stories about their sons and daughters, and spouses interrupt to set the record straight about what really happened because one obviously got it all wrong. Just imagine the howl of protest if one family member tried to write the definitive history of the family. Each member would *know* the real story had not been told and would tell anyone who would listen how it really was.

Consider all the commentaries and books written to interpret what is said in the Bible. Differences abound, depending on which author we read. The Bible contains a number of verses that lead many Christians to believe that the only path to unity with God is through Jesus Christ. Many well-meaning Christians believe that God loves all people, no matter what faith, but they cannot get past those references that tend to say that if a person does not believe that Jesus is the only Son of God, that person is not part of the select who will inherit eternal life. This exclusive view of the revelation of God causes great anxiety among Christians, and it requires believers to compete with other revelations in order to save the souls of the lost. This competition has been and will continue to be divisive and destructive to the unity of all God's children. To ameliorate this animosity and antagonism we search for another way to read the scriptures.

One example of a troubling passage is John 14:6. The author of John reports Jesus proclaimed, "I am the way, and the truth, and the life. No one comes to the Father except through me" (NSRV). A note of explanation at the bottom of the page says this passage means that "Access to God is solely through Jesus." To most, this means that for anyone to receive God's favor and eternal bliss, he/she must believe that Jesus is God's only Son and that Jesus is, indeed, the same as God. Believing this interpretation keeps Christians from embracing people of other faiths as truly equal members of the community of God. We are taught to feel that we must try to convert them to Christianity out of love for them, for if we don't convince them of the error of their ways, they are doomed to spend eternity out of the presence of God. When we express the belief to people of other faiths, most are offended and turn away with a very negative opinion of Christianity and the competition escalates.

However, there are other ways to interpret this text. We could say that Jesus meant that His life represented a life in right relationship with God. He eschewed material goods for spiritual ones. He lived humbly and loved His enemies. He talked with outcasts and dined with sinners to give them hope for a better life. His reason for being was to bring hope to those in despair. He prayed and meditated on God's Kingdom and tried to convince others to give up their selfish and destructive lifestyles. Following His example was the only means to a meaningful and deep relationship with the Divine. All the reading and studying and bickering over how to worship and what are orthodox and accepted beliefs pale in importance when compared to the example of Jesus' life and message.

When seen in this light, we may read Matthew 28:19 with new meaning. When Jesus says "Go therefore and make disciples of all nations, baptizing them in the name of the Father and of the Son and of the Holy Spirit, and teaching them to obey everything that I have commanded you," He may be saying that His teachings will change the world for the better and we must spread the word for the sake of all humanity. The cornerstone of Jesus' message is heard in Matthew 5:43, "You have heard that it was said, 'You shall love your neighbor and hate your enemy.' But I say to you, love your enemies and pray for those who persecute you, so that you may be children of your Father in heaven." We must stop hoarding the world's wealth to the detriment of others. We must share with the orphan, the widow, and the disabled. This may be what Jesus meant when He exhorted us to make disciples of all nations. Such an interpretation of this reading seems to be more congruous with Jesus' message and allows us to embrace all our neighbors truly as brothers and sisters. When we restrict access to God to those who accept Jesus as His only true son, we exclude so many people who had little or no chance to be part of the movement, let alone those who, though well educated in matters of scripture, come to different conclusions than those in positions of religious authority. Think of all the people living at the time of Jesus in parts of the world unknown to the Romans and the disciples. Are these souls lost? Think of all the people who lived and died for centuries in places on Earth where Jesus' name was never spoken. What of the souls living since then that grew up loving God in other traditions? Their parents, grandparents and ancestors worshipped in ways that resonate in their very being. They lead lives completely compatible with Jesus' teaching, and yet because they cannot accept a foreign practice, they are doomed? If we do say God can love and accept those who through no fault of their own never heard of Jesus, why can we not accept the religious who choose to worship God in other traditions? Is it possible that we truly cannot understand, even through faith-based study of our culturally accepted scripture, God's thoughts in their entirety? Consider the implications for Christians as the prophet Isaiah shares the Word of God in Isaiah 55: 8-9, "For my thoughts are not your thoughts, nor are your ways my ways, says the Lord. For as the heavens are higher than the earth, so are my ways higher than your ways and my thoughts than your thoughts."

The Bible should never be used as a weapon to beat down those who disagree with us. It should be used to further God's Kingdom here on Earth. We interpret that Kingdom as including all people who truly work for a more just, humane world. Rabbi Sandi Eisenberg Sasso said, in an article published in the *Indianapolis Star* in 1999, "You don't have to take the Bible literally to take it seriously." By that we think she meant that there are timeless truths contained in scripture, and to believe them you do not have to believe in the literal truth of every story or verse. Jesus, in Mark 12:28, when asked which commandment is the first of all answered, "The first is, Hear, O Israel: the Lord our God, the Lord is one; you shall love the Lord your God with all your heart, and with all your soul, and with all your mind, and with all your strength. The second is this; you shall love your neighbor as yourself. There is no other commandment greater than these." These are indeed timeless truths.

Perhaps we do risk being dismissed as just two more in a long line of individuals wishing to portray Jesus as a "great moral teacher," putting forth a soft "anything goes" theology without meeting the demands of real faith. To do so misses our point. We are not trying to reduce Christianity or any other religion to such a least common denominator, but rather we seek to understand how and why the "demands of real faith" developed. Once understood in a wider context, it is then up to the individual to choose what "truth" speaks to that individual. C.S. Lewis is widely quoted as saying that Jesus either was who He said He was, or else He was a lunatic. This opinion, however, stems from a subjective understanding of the Bible that is not universally embraced. Interpreting the scripture in a literal manner effectively draws a line in the sand and forces such an either/or conclusion. Again, perhaps the Christian belief that Christ was both human and divine actually offers a way out of this dilemma. The divine nature of Christ may resonate with those who have received this gift of faith, whereas His human nature and/or eternal spirit may resonate with others. Accepting such paradoxes allows one to embrace the simple beauty of the gift in nonexclusive ways. Furthermore just by believing that Jesus was the Son of God it does not necessarily follow (if one believes there is some validity to the observations discussed previously) that all traditional doctrine must be accepted in order to be true to demands of "real" faith. Furthermore, accepting the timeless *truth* of Christ as our savior, but evaluating such acceptance in light of numerous uncertainties (God's origin, complete nature, and thoughts? Biblical authority?) offers up the possibility that such truth might be understood in nontraditional and nonexclusive ways. This ultimately is the key point we seek to impress upon our readers. If persuaded that authority and truth are to be seen in relative terms, then it is our contention that believers from diverse faiths will be empowered to reach out to others in a manner previously impossible due to human limitations placed on the process. As stated previously it is not our intention to persuade the reader to accept our beliefs on any specific issue or to deny any cherished beliefs of one's own. Recognize, however, that the rationale for any of our beliefs is not so completely infallible as to be beyond questioning. Our beliefs need not be professed in such absolute terms so as to preclude the possibility that another's *truth* may have validity as well. There are many legitimate questions raised not meaning to be confrontational, but rather to experience the dialogue from which all of us can advance our spiritual journeys and achieve a deeper sense of connection with God and others. From this perspective we are called upon to evaluate our beliefs in a new light. Questioning interpretations of the Torah, Qur'an, or Bible becomes a responsibility, and we find that "truth" takes on new dimensions.

Before moving on to further discussion about truth itself, a more contentious issue needs to be addressed. Does our questioning the absolute authority of sacred scriptures jeopardize the foundation of our moral codes? Are claims of moral superiority just statements of self-serving personal preference? Can we deny the existence of absolute truth without opening the door to moral anarchy? We have already offered some comments in this regard in the introduction but feel some additional explanation is warranted. Perhaps our answers to such questions are too simplistic, but we will share them nevertheless. First, though the discussion in this chapter may suggest to some that we deny absolute authority and therefore absolute truth, such an inference is not our intention. We believe absolute truths do indeed exist in a religious context and such truths are shared by most religions that have passed the test of time (to be discussed in detail in Chapter VII). Adherence to these truths transcends the competition amongst religions to defend their relative truths and moral claims. Those truths shared by the great religions provide the standard, the framework, from which to judge human behavior. Ultimately our actions reflect our own personal or religious beliefs, and we would suggest that an omnipresent God either maintains a potential (i.e. we have to choose to accept God's presence) influence on the development of our moral code; or, considering the alternate viewpoint of the atheist, our moral code has been born of the experience and reason of people whose moral and ethical dilemmas are in constant flux with innate human nature, both good and evil. Our studies and contemplation as outlined in this chapter relative to the writing and interpretation of scripture lead us to the conclusion that if God does indeed exist, then it does *not* necessarily follow that all of our moral constructs are direct and immutable products of such scripture. The questions we raise relative to the Bible are germane to discussion of any sacred scripture. It is only because of our cultural upbringing that we focus on the Bible while raising these issues. We caution the Christian reader to not take such questions personally or consider our viewpoints to be anti-Christian. To the contrary we have tried to share with you our belief that the Bible is a wonderful living document full of many timeless truths that are part of the fabric of our morality and spirituality and our means to connect with God. But like any living organism, we believe this document, as well as other sacred scriptures, can adapt to its environment and change with time. We have cited examples of how this has been so in the past and present, and we can only presume it will continue in the future. The simple beauty of the Bible is such that it will survive the adaptations of the evolution of religion, and it will be symbiotic with others also adapting to cultural change. Perhaps it is this simple beauty of the Bible and Jesus' message that Rick Warren and others primarily wish to promote. Such an effort is laudable and should be appreciated for the focus it may help us achieve living in a stressful world. But please don't take it out of context. Christians and Christianity don't exist in a vacuum. Considering the role of the Bible and Jesus from a wider worldview will advance us closer to the endgame.

DISCUSSION QUESTIONS

1) Do apparent contradictions or inconsistencies in the Bible bother me in any way?

2) Has God's "personality" seemed to evolve through the centuries?

3) If I believe some "facts" in the Bible are in error, then what are the implications for other controversial passages?

4) Can more than one interpretation be valid? Who decides?

5) What does it mean to me when I hear it said that Jesus was human and divine? Does the human nature allow for some "flaws" or does it just refer to a physical presence in human form?

6) What are the implications of authority and truth being evaluated in relative terms?

CHAPTER V

TRUTH: RELATIVE OR ABSOLUTE?

" I preach there are all kinds of truth, your truth, and somebody
else's. But behind all of them there is only one truth and that is
that there is no truth."

Flannery O'Connor, in <u>Wise Blood</u>

Truth is a very tricky word. It is used in many different ways
and is easily misunderstood by both speakers and listeners. The
American Heritage Dictionary has fourteen variations of usage
for the word *true*. Philosophers try to define it and still it eludes
definition. Mortimer Adler wrote an essay about it in his book
<u>Ten Philosophical Mistakes,</u> and he tried to clarify what it means
and how it is supposed to be used. Clarity is very important when
discussing matters of faith. Misunderstandings are certain to arise
if we don't know precisely what someone means when a word is
used, especially a word that implies as much authority as "truth"

does. Professor Adler says that the concept of truth must be tied to certainty and knowledge. "When the criteria for calling anything knowledge are such exacting criteria as the certitude, incorrigibility, and immutability of the truth that is known, then the few things that are knowledge stand far apart from everything that might be called opinion. Examples of knowledge in the extreme sense of the term are a small number of self-evident truths. A self-evident truth is one that states something the opposite of which it is impossible to think." He goes on to cite a few examples that meet those criteria such as "a triangle has no nonadjacent angles." Of course, not many bits of knowledge can meet these demands, but that doesn't mean everything else is mere opinion rather than truth. But it does mean we have to be very careful when we use the word. We have to know in what context we are using it and what body of knowledge supports naming it as truth. If the verifiable knowledge is sketchy or based upon texts which can be questioned or contradicted by other texts of equal or similar reliability, then we must expect that other reasonable people will disagree. These dissenters are not evil or corrupt, necessarily. They simply see the evidence differently and draw other conclusions. Labeling a thing true because we believe it, regardless of a lack of hard evidence, or even contradicting evidence or opinions, renders the word less exclusive and leaves the door open for other truths about the same subject that meet the same standard for evidence but disagree with the original truth.

With such caution in mind, we wonder if the word *truth* even belongs in our discussion of religion. We have already discussed the lack of certainty we have that God inspired the writing of the entire

Bible or that what is written represents the *only* revelation from God. We mean certainty in the sense that it is verifiable by the usual sort of analysis and scholarship. In Chapter IV we discussed some of the problems with close analysis of Biblical texts. Authorship is uncertain, meaning of words and context are vague, contradictions occur, and theology is uneven. Given these conditions, another word other than truth might be more appropriate.

Perhaps beliefs, or teachings, or some other less exclusive term could convey the meaning without the implied absolute infallibility and inflexibility. We are not splitting hairs by proposing this change in terminology. Words matter a great deal in religion. The Jews were called the "People of the Book" by their neighbors for a reason. They studied and analyzed every single word in the Torah and other ancient writings. But words matter not only to those inside the faith community but also to those outside. If we can be less threatening to those outside the faith by the words we use, we stand a better chance of entering into dialogue and reaching mutual respect and understanding. If we preface what we say with the words, "It is my belief...," we open the door to dialogue. If we preface our remarks with, "The truth is...," we close that door.

Using the word *truth* to describe our religious beliefs conveys a sense of certainty about the knowledge we possess. Many Christians say that belief in Jesus Christ, as the Son of God, is the only way to attain eternal salvation. They say Jesus must be accepted as a divine being just as God is; in fact, as part of God or the same as God. This is part of the mystery of the Trinity: all human, all divine; part of God, but separate. They call this the truth of the Gospels.

However, we cannot prove this by any corroborating source outside the Gospels. There are many who believe it and restate it and affirm it, but nowhere other than the Gospels is there any indisputable evidence of it. There is no body of evidence outside the Gospels to *prove* Jesus rose from the dead. There are no verifiable sources to attest to Jesus' appearance to the disciples after His death. For those of a particular predisposition Jesus' resurrection *is* verifiable in a religious sense but recognize that this is different than academic, historical, or scientific validation. Though it is our opinion that there is insufficient verification by these parameters, this should not be construed as saying that such beliefs lack validity or applicability in today's world. However it is crucial that any of us critically evaluate the reasons *why* we ultimately reach a particular belief and consider it as truth. Christians accept such beliefs on faith. They have faith in the Gospels, in their church, and in their traditions passed down over many generations. The lack of evidence does not mean the claims are false, but it does make the use of the word *truth* potentially confrontational.

Professor Adler said that for something to be true there should be a body of evidence or knowledge that makes any other conclusion incomprehensible, or at least illogical. Such is not the case with these or any religious beliefs. Certain knowledge of the divine is not possible. We cannot know the unknowable. No one can claim absolute certainty about who God is or the totality of God's thought processes. We can *believe* certain things, but we cannot *know* them to be true, if we use Professor Adler's definition of knowledge. If we don't use his definition, but another one that is less exacting, then we must grant that others can also use it for opposing views without being labeled as false or untrue. Therefore, there can be many "truths" without necessarily implying conflict or contradiction.

We can search the ancient and modern texts, meditate, pray, talk with others and still we only see and understand a small part of this mystery. We search all our lives and we cannot bridge the gap between divine and human. That doesn't mean the divine doesn't exist or that it is futile to search. The search produces wonderful results. We benefit from great writings by some of the world's foremost minds. We learn about great lives filled with selfless acts and sacrifices made from loyalty to the ideals of Jesus and Mohammed and Buddha and others. The cause of social justice is enhanced because of these ideals. People are fed, clothed, educated, adopted, and cherished by what would otherwise be strangers because of the examples we read about in the sacred texts.

The point is, however, that one religion cannot trump another with the claim that it is the sole possessor of God's truth. This inability to trump does not diminish the cause of religion at all. A few religions make the claim of exclusivity of revelation for a number of reasons. One of the most prominent though is the fate of the soul for eternity. Most Christians believe that a person's fate for eternity hinges upon his or her belief or non-belief that Jesus is the only, divine Son of God. This is the ticket to heaven or hell. Where a person spends eternity is based on accepting the free gift of God's grace given through Jesus Christ. No amount of good deeds, no amount of kindness or humility, no selfless act can earn a person entry into heaven -- only the belief in Jesus described here can do that. With such dire consequences predicted for unbelievers, the believers are exhorted to make disciples (defined believers) of all nations and peoples for their own salvation. We understand the altruistic nature of this cause, but we question whether it is grounded in sound thinking about who God is and what God's sense of justice is for all people. The religious playing field is not level. Christianity is very natural and easy for people born in certain areas of the world. It is part of the fabric of America, for instance. We grow up hearing about Jesus from very early in our lives, even if our families are not religious. He is all over the airwaves, both television and radio. He is in the movies and in literature. We debate about prayer to Him in schools. We have church camps for our youth, campus crusades on college campuses and on and on. It is almost unthinkable for many westerners that we would be anything other than Christian. Our parents and grandparents practiced the faith and took us to church. Our presidents and politicians invoke God's name on public occasions. What else would we be? What other belief system would we embrace? It is so easy for us.

What about those born in parts of the globe where Christianity is an alien or an even unknown faith? What of those whose parents and grandparents read to them from the Qur'an, or the Bhagavad-Gita, or the teachings of the Buddha? For centuries and for generations these families developed traditions and experiences related to these "other" religious practices. They try to follow the teachings of their leaders or their God. They lead exemplary lives. They live, suffer and die devoted to their beliefs. Will God exclude them from eternal salvation because they refuse to turn their backs on their faith (their gift from God?), the faith of their families and their entire culture? We don't think so. It seems unlikely God would put so many obstacles in so many people's path and then condemn them for not overcoming them. Of course, some people in these other cultures convert to Christianity. But some devout Christians, also uncomfortable with this dilemma, explain that these people will most likely have the opportunity after their human death to know and accept Jesus. Such conjecture preserves their belief in the accuracy of Bible accounts stating all will come to God through Jesus Christ. We have to acknowledge, though, that Christians also convert to other religions. Who can say why one set of teachings reaches one person when another does not? This seems to point to the old saying that "one size does not fit all."

Some of the world's great religions acknowledge this phenomenon. In Hinduism a great sage known as Ramakrishna said, "Mother, Mother, Mother! Everyone foolishly assumes that his clock alone tells correct time. Christians claim to possess exclusive truth... Countless varieties of Hindus insist that their sect, no matter how small and insignificant, expresses the ultimate position. Devout Muslims maintain that Koranic revelation supersedes all others. The entire world is being driven insane by this single phrase: 'My religion alone is true.' O Mother, you have shown me that no clock is entirely accurate. Only the transcendent sun of knowledge remains on time. Who can make a system from Divine Mystery? But if any sincere practitioner, within whatever culture or religion, prays and meditates with great devotion and commitment to Truth alone, Your Grace will flood his mind and heart, O Mother. His particular sacred tradition will be opened and illuminated. He will reach the one goal of spiritual evolution. Mother, Mother, Mother! How I long to pray with sincere Christians in their churches and to bow and prostrate with devoted Muslims in their mosques! All religions are glorious!"

Similarly, in the Qur'an it is written in Surah 14:4 "We never sent a messenger except with the language of his people, so that he might make [the message] clear for them." In Mark, Chapter 12, Jesus says the greatest commandments are to love God and love our neighbors. He did not say to love only those who believe like you. That was evident in the story of the Good Samaritan. He said to love without reservation. We believe part of loving is accepting differences and celebrating them. To just tolerate others is not enough. Tolerance, even if offered in a humble and conciliatory manner, implies superiority. Inherent to this mentality is an insidious air of righteousness, which the discerning "other" will ultimately resent and resist. We don't need to require agreement on all matters of faith to embrace each other as brothers and sisters. In fact, it could be said that the struggle for agreement, rather than contributing to harmony and understanding, divides and separates us.

Human nature seems to lend credence to the thought that agreement on matters of faith will never happen. Look at examples from other disciplines. In medicine, genetic makeup of a particular patient affects the type and dosage of medication that may be indicated for certain conditions. What will cure or help one person can harm or kill another. In parenting, we see that what motivates one child humiliates and destroys another. The accomplished classroom teacher recognizes that some children learn by reading, others by hearing, and still others by touch or experience. We are not all the same. Each of us brings personality, experience, family, intelligence, and countless other variables to the altar of our faith. It is entirely reasonable that some of us require spiritual disciplines different than our neighbors. Animosity and enmity do not need to flow from such differences. We can learn so much from one another if we open ourselves to acceptance and celebration of our siblings of other faiths.

This does not mean love the sinner, hate the sin. Nor does it suggest we love the unbeliever, but convince him to believe. That attitude will not bring us together on the journey to God. Others have suggested, and we are certainly in no position to argue, that God will ultimately decide the questions of eternity: who gets eternal life and who doesn't. There are so many unanswered questions about God that we don't feel any of us can be responsible for the fate of others. We as believers must trust that God's sense of justice will prevail. Jesus preached about helping the poor, the widow and the less fortunate more than any other subject. We can bring this message of God to people here and now. How can we improve life among all people? How can we bring a sense of God's Kingdom here to Earth for all to experience? Jesus talked of peace. He prized peace for all His children. We can be vehicles of that peace. We can preach His messages of love and social consciousness. He wanted us to care about each other and feel each other's pain and share in each other's joy. He taught us to look at life differently than it is our nature to do. In the Sermon on the Mount, He tried to lead us to the reality that the important things in life are not possessions or power or status, but relationship with God and with each other.

Huston Smith, in the conclusion of his book <u>The World's Religions,</u> wrote, "Not all of their [the world's religions] contents are enduringly wise. Modern science has superseded their cosmologies, and the social mores of their day, which they reflect -- gender relations, class structures and the like -- must be reassessed in the light of changing times and the continuing struggle for justice. But if we pass a strainer through the world's religions to lift out their conclusions about reality and how life should be lived, those conclusions begin to look like the winnowed wisdom of the human race."

For us, Christianity provides our spiritual home. We feel at home with Jesus and His teachings. They speak to us. We feel connected to our past through participation in His church. We know of no better place to express our yearning to be part of something larger than ourselves. Hearing the message of Jesus week after week keeps us focused on "the better angels of our nature," instead of being consumed by selfishness and narcissistic pursuits. We want our children to know that ethics, social justice, morality and caring for others are noble pursuits, worthy of our time and efforts. If we can somehow set aside our insistence on the existence of "one true religion," the possibilities seem endless. If we could genuinely prostrate ourselves with the Muslim and pray with Hindu, think of the brotherhood and sisterhood that could result. If we sat down with the Buddhist and listened with no thought of trying to convince him of the superior merits of Christianity, think of the things we could learn. Think of what we could teach in return. Eastern religions seem so advanced in matters of prayer and connection with the divine. Would we not all benefit by sitting at their feet and learning the benefits of such methods? Such dialogue is only possible if we do not insist upon the superiority of our own beliefs. We, in turn, could tell them why the Sermon on the Mount and the parables of Jesus move us so profoundly. We could tell them how our experience of God through Jesus challenges us to look for ways to improve the lot of the lost and forgotten of the world.

Much of the religious experience is personal and has little to do with dogma or doctrine. We want to feel connected to something that matters and that is larger than ourselves. It is hard to deny the yearning felt across cultural and social boundaries for a spiritual life. Meaningful dialogue across those boundaries, unfortunately, is often stifled by religious competition. Each exclusive religion feels under attack and threatened by the others. They warn their adherents against the evil infidels of other lands and cultures. They promote fear and trembling by listing all the insidious acts perpetrated by the various others who choose to exploit and misrepresent religious doctrine in the pursuit of power. This practice has gone on for centuries and continues unabated today. Wars, economic exploitation, prejudice and strife are the sad consequences of such attitudes.

We feel one way to break the cycle of distrust and fear is to trust God and welcome other religions as equal partners in the endeavor to bring about God's Kingdom here on Earth. We may offer the opinion that God will judge the merits of all our hearts at the time of final judgment, but in so doing we know that we risk alienating those who have unshakable belief in the Christian concept of grace received through acceptance of Jesus Christ. For us, though it may seem paradoxical to some, we do not feel that *belief* in the concept of grace necessarily implies *knowing* that God mandates its acceptance universally in order to receive salvation. God's complete nature is just too difficult for us to comprehend. We certainly can receive great comfort in understanding those aspects of God revealed to us through our cultural experiences and spiritual revelations, but we cannot escape the feeling that there is more to the story, that the understanding to which we are privy is but just a small (but individually significant) part of "the divine mosaic." We cannot prove that the paradox of being comfortable with accepting conflicting *truths* is part of God's plan, but in light of the preceding discussions, is acceptance of this paradox any less rational than any absolute adherence to a single ultimate truth? It is our contention that if our ultimate goal is to lead a life reflecting the teachings of Jesus, then acceptance of the paradox is indeed more rational, and we all will be better served by adhering to this principle.

Discussion Questions

1) What does the word "truth" imply to me? What do I think it means to others?

2) What determines whether we *know* something to be true or whether we *believe* it to be true?

3) Do I believe all competing truths necessarily are mutually exclusive?

CHAPTER VI

EVOLUTION OF GOD: INSULT OR PROGRESS?

Wherever we are, it is but a stage on the way to somewhere else, and whatever we do, however well we do it, it is only a preparation to do something else that shall be different.

Robert Louis Stevenson

Your mind cannot possibly understand God. Your heart already knows. Minds were designed for carrying out the orders of the heart.

Emmanuel

If our discussion in the preceding chapters has led you at least to consider new and different ways of approaching traditional religious thought and practice, then we feel there is no limit to what God can do toward our stated goal of global acceptance of diversity.

Once the bonds of doctrinal narcissism are broken, we are freed to pursue the real purpose of religion. Our atheist friends tell us life is conferred meaning by nurturing relationships with others. Bishop Spong contends that happiness is found when we seek the happiness and well being of others, and this is inherently good whereas it is inherently wrong to seek to cause or increase the pain of another. Religions provide a valued framework for enhancing our relationship with God and fellow man by establishing, as Rabbi Kushner defines it, a structure for communities of seekers of truth: those seeking understanding of the world and our role in it, seeking fellowship and support, seeking understanding of God. Though questions abound on matters of doctrine, we have little cause to question the goodness manifest by our religious communities when it comes to matters of charity. What other community or organization dedicates itself so totally to trying to "do the right thing," promoting the happiness and well being of others? It is the lives and actions of involved individuals that reflect the presence of God in our lives. Though we may differ widely in our definition of this presence, and the resulting doctrines, what we do know is that it feels right to help others. Whether God-given or otherwise, this feeling is as real as countless other emotions such as love or anger, which though they may not be explainable by our five senses or with mathematical proofs or scientific reason, are accepted as valid parts of our being. Being true to this feeling, choosing to reflect the spirit of good which resides in all of us is the ultimate form of worshipping God. We cannot presume to understand God's intentions, but we can feel a divine presence as well as a sense of pride in being part of a community that serves, heals, nurtures, and inspires others regardless of their race, gender, socioeconomic status, sexual orientation or theology. This, we feel, is the mandate of the "God presence" within our lives. It is following our inner voice that receives direction and form from a force unknowable in absolute terms to us of human limitations. There is a satisfaction that comes from doing what is right during this finite time we have on earth, not because we have a faith that promises salvation or eternal life, but simply because the conscious choice to embrace honesty rather than deceit, good rather than evil, acceptance rather than self-serving intolerance, compassion rather than indifference, is inherently good.

Though many religious leaders are strong advocates for tolerance within religion, the same tolerance may not be extended to those who define themselves outside religion. Numerous philosophers and theologians have offered their description of what would be the abhorrent nature of a godless world, and Rabbi Kushner even contends, in a manner we find particularly disheartening, "The atheist is not the person who denies the existence of God, but the one who denies the value of love, courage, and honesty." Can such an opinion be supported by our own experience with atheists? Many describe a world of cruelty and selfishness if there were no God. History leaves little doubt, however, that the presence of God does not protect us from such human frailties. God's presence does not force us to choose good over evil; nor would God's absence necessitate the converse. The human condition encompasses the whole spectrum of qualities including love, honesty, courage, cruelty, and selfishness.

Does anyone really believe that if there were no God we could just redefine "good" to inherently include greed, cruelty, and hedonism? Does that *feel* right? We cannot prove that this would not occur, but don't all of us, including Kushner, know atheists who embody good living much more so than many of their believer counterparts? If one believes that these "good" atheists are just those under the influence of an unacknowledged God, then we are just back to the point that dogma is not of critical importance, but that God's power transcends belief versus non-belief.

Now perhaps the atheists among you are reading this and thinking this entire discussion to be merely rationalization to allow for belief in a supreme being with the promise of eternal life. All of this is just a product of generations of emotionally weak humans unable to accept their own mortality. You could be right, but can you, or will anyone ever be able to, *know* this to be true? Can you ever know this with certainty, requiring of yourself the same criteria of proof you would demand of a devout believer trying to prove the existence of God? How can you prove, even in your own mind, the nonexistence of something when you live in a world of infinite dimension but you come to your opinions from a limited set of experiences? Perhaps it is time for all of us to soften the rhetoric of extreme positions. Choosing either extreme in matters of theological debate results in a line of separation from others, closing the door to free dialogue, invalidating the opinions of others as mere rationalizations. What is to be gained from such a hard-line position? Isn't there some degree of hypocrisy in condemning the opinions of those who hold extreme *beliefs*, all the while professing an absolute commitment to one's own exclusive *truth*? Making responsible choices isn't about securing eternal life; it's about understanding who we are and what we can do to promote the common good, without being divisive, condescending, or harmful to others.

In fact, it would appear that if there is no other life than this earthly one, then choices we make become all the more important. If we have no "second chance," then we better do what is "right and good" the first time around. It matters not from where the inherent good arose but rather just that it is, and we can choose whether to embrace it. In his book Who Needs God, Rabbi Kushner does not address the issue of whether or not God truly exists, but rather he explores the question of why God is important. So also we should not get caught up in arguments over whether inherent good exists but rather understand why it is important. The presence of inherent good, a conscience with a moral compass, allows us to not be exclusionary in our respective theologies. There is little to be gained from ostracizing or alienating atheists or any others who may choose to adhere to a set of religious beliefs which may be in conflict with our own; nor is such a position consistent with the universal presence of a limitless God who is the fabric of our everyday existence. Every moment can be a "God moment" if we invoke God's presence, but we must *choose* to do so. In the Biblical story recounting the choice God gave man in the Garden of Eden, it is said that Adam and Eve chose to partake of the apple and have knowledge of good and evil. This knowledge, coupled with reason and experience, amounts to free will and demands choice. Granted, it is not always clear which choice may most accurately reflect the spirit of God, but we live in a world with many shades of gray, not always black and white. The challenges of situational ethics and matters of morality contribute to the uniquely human flavor of our existence. As long as our opinions reflect a thought process ripe with love, courage, honesty, and compassion the choices we make will reflect the spirit of God emanating from within us.

Defining purpose in life, Islamic teaching advocates social responsibility unified under one God with all duties and activities religious-based. Rick Warren is similar in his theology stating simply, "It is all about God," and God is to be present in each and every moment, guiding every decision. Secularism is seen as deviating from God's path, denying God's presence, and rendering society at risk for chaos. Perhaps there is more overlap between secular aspects of society and God-based activities than is generally appreciated. Each of us can choose to invoke God's presence even in seemingly secular activities. Even a "secular" event cannot be devoid of an *omnipresent* God, but God-based does not necessarily mean religion-based. When our founding fathers advocated separation of church and state, they did so in order to prohibit the establishment of any single state religion. They vigorously defended the right of individuals to exercise their own beliefs, but not to the exclusion of others. Some have suggested that all-inclusive concepts of God, whether personal of impersonal, seemed to be acceptable to the writers of the Declaration as they made reference to "divine Providence." Doesn't acceptance of religion as a means for us to reflect "divine Providence" put religion, and associated doctrines, in proper perspective? Mohammed speaking on the issue of equality in the Hadith states, "All people are equal, as equal as the teeth of a comb. An Arab is no better than a non-Arab, nor is a white person over a black person, nor is the male superior to the female. The only people who enjoy preference with God are the devout." Are not the truly devout those who in fact treat others as equals, those who are God-conscious and try to reflect God's presence in their daily interactions with others, friend and foe alike, regardless of religious affiliation?

It has been the followers of Jesus and Mohammed who have been so inspired as to portray their teachings as final revelations, the last word of God, but did Jesus or Mohammed ever claim this themselves? In chapters IV and V, we have already questioned the certainty with which any of us could reach such a conclusion. Furthermore we have suggested that arguing over the answer to such issues only serves to block the path to unity. Instead might we not appreciate that the presence and power of their messages influential still today serves as affirmation of the history-altering religious experience that occurred centuries ago? Hopefully, if you have stuck with us thus far in our discussions, it won't be difficult to accept the suggestion that like any exceptional teachers (regardless of whether you believe Jesus to be divine or Mohammed directly in communication with Allah), they would have wanted to teach not only a moral way of life for their contemporaries, but more importantly, would have sought to teach principles of moral living which would transcend the generations. Is not this their greatest gift to us? Though traditional Christians might suggest Jesus' dying on the cross for forgiveness of our sins was the single greatest gift from

119

God, we must remember that we are dealing with different realms when we refer to the Christian "us" versus the collective, global "us." When Jesus states in the Gospel of John that "No one comes to the Father except through me," He doesn't say to His disciples that they would eventually have to recite and literally believe all yet-to-be-compiled Christian creeds. We discussed this passage previously in chapter IV but feel it is so crucial as to deserve further emphasis. Could Jesus have meant that we will not experience God fully unless we follow the path exemplified by Jesus through His life and message? Application of the scriptural teachings allows us to feel the comfort, joy, love, compassion and sense of community Jesus felt. If we use the gifts available to us to enter selflessly into relationship with others, are we not coming to God through Jesus Christ? The apostle Paul in Romans 2:9-11, and 13-16 (NRS) expands on this universal theme stating, "There will be anguish and distress for everyone who does evil, the Jew first and also the Greek, but glory and honor and peace for *everyone* who does good, the Jew first and also the Greek. For God shows *no partiality...* for it is not the bearers of the law who are righteous in God's sight, but the doers of the law who will be justified. When Gentiles who do not possess the law, do *instinctively* what the law requires, these, though not having the law are a law to themselves. They show that what the law requires is written in their hearts, to which their own conscience also bears witness and their conflicting thoughts will accuse or excuse them on the day when according to my gospel, God, through Jesus Christ, will judge the secret thoughts of all." Likewise Muslims in addressing the fate of unbelievers support the idea that the final judgment is up to God (Qur'an 2:62). We believe the time has come for us, of limited human experience and perspective, to quit being judgmental over issues of doctrine and individual choice. Rick Warren, though expressing confidence in *knowing* what God thinks and wants to a degree that we find very discomforting, makes an excellent point acknowledging God embracing diversity while at the same time noting that we indeed are products of our own environment and experiences: "...the music style you like says more about you -- your background and personality -- than it does about God. One ethnic group's music can sound like noise to another. But God likes variety and enjoys it *all*." Cannot we see the same is true for religion? If God put Jews, Muslims, Christians, Buddhists, Hindus...atheists on this world, doesn't God enjoy them all? Isn't Jewish doctrine "noise" to the Muslim, but doesn't God embrace both? If my Muslim brother were raised by my Jewish family, wouldn't he be a Jew? Doesn't my "religious style" say more about me -- my background and personality -- then it does about the absolute total nature of God? Does not in fact the whole human nature of God, the human style in which we portray God, reflect more about us than God? An old folk story suggests that if horses had gods they would look like horses. Are we suggesting that man created God in his own image? As an atheist, sure, this may be a logical, intellectual conclusion if one limits oneself to a single perspective. But can atheists *know* this to be true, supported by scientific *fact* or do they *believe* this because it feels right, because this conclusion is consistent with *their* experience and reason?

But what about the theist who actually may have created God in his own image? Are we just rationalizing the existence of God so as to avoid the emotional upheaval that would accompany the admission that much of the foundation of our society and morality has been based upon a self-serving delusion? This hypothesis, though perhaps not unreasonable to some, cannot be proven by any scientific facts, nor does the human character of God necessitate accepting any philosophical argument that God is just a delusional product of man's needs. If God exists, and the infinite nature and intentions of God cannot be known to us by virtue of our own limitations, then why shouldn't God "...create man in His own image" (though perhaps not the only image) and vice versa? Our image of God tells us a great deal about the nature of human beings, but it does not logically follow that the full nature of God is revealed in humanity alone. Nor can one conclude from scripture that the "image" referred to is that of physical image. Thomas Aquinas in *Summa Theologica* explains this passage as referring to our being infused with the ethical and moral image of God. Ethical and moral behaviors consistent with a God presence are certainly not limited to those who hold to a particular theology.

To put limits on the unknown cannot be justified by any scientific or philosophical argument. What one *feels* as a theist requires no more justification then justifying the love any of us feel for our families or committed life partner. No equations, regardless of how many variables may be factored in, will ever explain or capture the essence of our love. Do we need to justify the reasons why relationships and a sense of community are important to us? We believe the existence of these feelings serve us well. Does this make them self-serving delusions? Or does their mere existence and their constancy throughout time and human nature lend credence to their validity? We cannot prove the existence of love any more than we can prove the existence of our concept of God, but we also can see no value in discarding either just because each might be self-serving "delusions," unless self-serving entails restricting our love of others to only those who share our same background and concept of God. Therein lies the danger of absolute systems of belief. Whether it be an atheist's absolute denial of the existence of God or a monotheist's strict adherence to religious doctrine, both are exclusionary; neither position promotes a dialogue or the development of healthy relationships which just may prove capable of adding new dimension to our lives. If the breadth of our human experience necessarily limits our concept of God, the God we "create," wouldn't we be smarter to embrace and try to understand the total human experience? If we, as Covey recommends in Seven Habits of Highly Effective People, begin with the end in mind, can we not agree on a reasonable endgame? Might this endgame involve the synthesis of a multitude of differing perspectives, embracing common goals, validating each other's experiences without being patronizing or simply tolerant? Would the pursuit of such a goal be an insult to God? Or is it progress? The obstacles need not be insurmountable for people committed to the same goal. Exploring the common ground of the world religions may advance our cause in this regard.

Discussion Questions

1) What is the role of religion in our society? What role does it play in my life?

2) Do I sense the presence of the divine in some way?

3) Do I believe human nature is inherently good, evil, or both? Why?

4) What do I *know* about the nature of God? Does it make sense to me that any single religion is fully capable of describing the exact will and nature of a God of infinite dimension?

5) If God's nature has evolved with the rise of human consciousness, then what vision of God's future nature might we collectively wish to embrace?

CHAPTER VII

THE BONDS THAT UNITE US

The world is not to be put in order, the world is order incarnate.
It is for us to put ourselves in unison with this order.

Henry Miller

Once having accepted the uncertainties pervasive in any
discussion involving matters of religion, we find deeper meaning
in the discovery of the common features amongst world religions.
The many similarities that suggest common origins and serve
to unite seemingly disparate systems of belief, when recognized
while humbly acknowledging that the total nature of God cannot
be known to any one individual or religion, help us to celebrate the
religious diversity of humankind. Friedrich Heiler, in his essay
"The History of Religion as a Preparation for the Co-operation of
Religion," outlines such similarities stating, "Innumerable parallels
between Christianity and other religions have been discovered

in recent decades by historians of religions. One really must say that there is no religious concept, no dogmatic teaching, no ethical demand, no churchly institution, no cultic form and practice of piety in Christianity that does not have diverse parallels in the non-Christian religions. Examples are the belief in the Trinity, in Creation, in Incarnation; the concepts of a virgin birth, vicarious suffering, the death and resurrection of the redeemer god; the inspiration of sacred scripture; the sole efficacy of grace; the forgiveness of sin; infused prayer; the imitation of God; the glory of paradise; the fulfilled kingdom of God; the priesthood and monasticism; sacraments and liturgical ceremonies, including the rosary. All these not only are Christian but are universally religious and universally human."

Joseph Campbell illustrated this point in his conversation with Bill Moyers in the series *Power of the Myth*, when he said, "The death and resurrection of a savior figure is a common motif in all of these legends. For example, in the story of the origin of maize, you have this benign figure who appears to the young boy in a vision, and gives him maize, and dies. The plant comes from his body. Somebody has had to die in order for life to emerge. I begin to see this incredible pattern of death giving rise to birth, and birth giving rise to death. Every generation has to die in order that the next generation can come."

This idea that death gives birth to life is also present in the Hindu tradition. Philip Novak, in The World's Wisdom, relates the story of a divine being, Purusha, sacrificing himself so the world can be born. It is a creation myth combined with the god-sacrifice to bestow life. It seems people all over the world view the divine as loving its creation so much that it willingly dies to perpetuate life.

A creation myth of the Maori people of New Zealand resembles the story in Genesis to a remarkable degree:

Io dwelt within the breathing-space of immensity.

The Universe was in darkness with water everywhere.

There was no glimmer of dawn, no clearness, no light.

And he began by saying these words,

'...Darkness become a light possessing darkness.'

And at once light appeared.

(He) then repeated those self-same words in this manner...

'Light, become a darkness-possessing light.'

And again an intense darkness supervened.

Then a third time He spake saying:

'Let there be one darkness above,

Let there be one darkness below...

Let there be one light above,

Let there be one light below...

A dominion of light,

A bright light.'

And now a great light prevailed.

(Io) then looked to the waters which compassed him about,

and spake a fourth time, saying:

'Ye waters of Tai-kama, be ye separate.

Heaven be formed.' Then the sky became suspended.

'Bring forth thou Tupua-horo-nuku.'

And at once the moving earth lay stretched abroad.

Miraculous birth stories also dot the religious landscape all over the world. We all know the Christmas story about Jesus' birth. The angel appeared to Mary and told her she would have a son, conceived by the Holy Spirit. But, do we know the legend of the Buddha's birth? Again, Philip Novak quotes the story:

"There lived once upon a time a king of the Shakyas, a scion of the solar race, whose name was Shuddhodana.... He had a wife who was called Great Maya. These two tasted of love's delights, and one day she conceived the fruit of her womb, but without any defilement.... Just before her conception she had a dream. A white elephant seemed to enter her body, but without causing her any pain...."

Appreciating the parallels described by Heiler offers us the opportunity to scratch beneath the surface of cultural differences and religious competition. We are all too familiar with the victims of religious persecution and zealotry, and the emotional and cultural chasms deepened by such. But if we probe deeper, we might find that we have more in common than we think. Huston Smith used the analogy of the appearance of human beings to describe this phenomenon. He said, "If we look at human beings, the first thing that strikes us is how different they are -- different heights, different shapes, different complexions -- and yet we know that underlying this manifold diversity, the structure of the human spine that holds all these bodies erect is surprisingly similar...But the intriguing -- more than intriguing, the important -- thing that has become ever more evident the longer I work with these traditions is that at the heart of all of them is what we might call a conceptual spine that is extraordinarily the same." Understanding and embracing the common conceptual framework amongst the world religions arms us with the emotional and intellectual building blocks to begin to bridge the cultural chasm.

We acknowledge that differences exist. Jews do not believe that Jesus is a divine being, and they do not believe he is the long-awaited Messiah. Muslims do not accept that Jesus was crucified. Christians believe that both Jews and Muslims are missing salvation by not believing that Jesus is the Son of God. Moreover, the three monotheistic religions described here do not appear to have much in common with the Eastern traditions of Hinduism, Buddhism and Confucianism, among others. For centuries, and indeed millennia, most adherents of these traditions have not seen past these differences. Christians felt alien in the presence of Muslims. They could see no cross or altar. Jews felt excluded in churches and mosques. Very little common ground could be found. Even though all three traced their roots to a wandering nomad named Abraham, they could not unite as brothers or even cousins. They could not even agree to disagree as members of the same family sometimes do. Impasse and even antagonism seemed the only choice.

Again, Huston Smith provides the language for a possible alternative to this dilemma. He says there is a "primordial tradition" that is the "font and spring of them all. But it takes on, as it were, different coloring as it enters into, and in ways is also the source of, differing civilizations." This means that the same source "spirit" or "being" or "impulse" propelled Moses, Jesus, Mohammed, the Buddha, and the other spiritual pioneers of the world. They could not resist the yearning they felt to go beyond the ordinary to the extraordinary, from the finite to the infinite. On the surface, these great leaders followed different paths to search for their respective "perfections," but there are similarities if we want to see them. Seven unifying principles of major religions are identified in Heiler's essay. Consideration of these principles will help us see the common ground our faiths share.

The first "area of unity" is "the reality of the transcendent, the holy, the divine, the Other." This reality can be called by many names: God, Allah, Yahweh, Jesus, Krishna, Vishnu, Goodness, Virtue and others. However expressed, the meaning is clear to the believers. It means there is some "Other" that we don't fully understand, but still we seek it.

This *reality* he considers to be self-evident for believers, stating as the second unifying principle: "This transcendent reality is immanent in human hearts. The divine spirit lives in all human souls." We feel it, but we don't quite know how to express it. In our most lucid or Spiritual moments, we feel called to be more than ourselves. We don't know why something moves us, but it does. It may be a butterfly or a smile of a stranger or a beautiful piece of music. We look at our children while they are sleeping, and we are overcome with a feeling so intense it can't be described. What is the source of this feeling? Is it the divine?

Third, "This reality is for man the highest good, the highest truth, righteousness, goodness, beauty..." We know there is a pure and true goodness to which we aspire. Sometimes it is hard to define and even harder to attain, but we still feel it is there.

Fourth, "This reality of the Divine is ultimate love which reveals itself to men and in men." Love is a key component of all major religions. This is not a coincidence. Love is the cornerstone of our efforts to be better than our selfish natures. We recognize that love is a positive response to the world's problems. It heals. It helps. It promotes other positives like justice, generosity and peace.

Fifth, "The way of man to God is universally the way of sacrifice. The path of salvation everywhere begins with sorrowful renunciation, resignation, the *via purgativa*, ethical self-discipline and asceticism. This path to God finds its continuation in meditation, contemplation and prayer." All of the major religions promote some sort of thoughtful communication with the Divine. It is a way to evaluate, consider, and call forth the Divine spark. The focus achieved helps to offset our imperfections and get our egos out of the way, ego and pride being two of the biggest obstacles to becoming the people of God.

Sixth, "All high religions teach not only the way to God, but always and at the same time the way to the neighbor as well. A neighbor is not merely every man without exception, but every living being. The mystic way of salvation is not completed in the *via comptemplativa*, in the 'flight of the alone to the alone' as Plotinus said (Enneadi. Vi. 9,11). Rather it finds its necessary continuation in service to the brother, the *vita activa*." This should be the most obvious of the principles of unity. In our deepest selves we know that helping our neighbors is an obligation we simply cannot ignore. Some are born to plenty and some are born to deprivation. Circumstances of birth are not a matter of choice, but we, who have been given so much by virtue of being born to plenty, can choose to share and be of service to those whose lives are difficult. The great religions all teach us to give of ourselves, and all of them extend this spirit of giving and love to include our enemies. Heiler shares with us many examples of Eastern and Western religions promoting this unifying (yet largely ignored today) principle: "One who becomes familiar with Buddhist lore is constantly struck by the purity, breadth, and depth of this love. But more astonishing still, this Buddhist love includes the love of the enemy, as also among Brahmans and Sufists...Loving the enemy has been commanded in India since the earliest times. We read in the heroic epic Mahabharata: 'Even an enemy must be afforded appropriate hospitality when he enters the house; a tree does not withhold its shade even from those who come to cut it down'...Buddha admonishes his disciples: 'Even if, O monks, robbers and murderers would sever one's members with a double-toothed saw, one by one, that person, if his spirit be filled with rage, would not be practicing my religion. Also in this case, then, you must beware: the mind must not be disturbed, we do not want to utter an evil word but remain kind and compassionate, well-intentioned, without inward hate; and we want to penetrate this human being with the spirit of goodness, with a boundless and immeasurable spirit free from hostility and ill-will.'...The Sufist Ibn Imad says: 'The perfect man shall render good to his enemies; for they do not know what they do. Thus he will be clothed with the qualities of God, for God always does good to his enemies even though they do not know him.'...The Jewish Chassidim also demand: 'In humility, the pious believer shall not return evil for evil, but forgive those who hate and persecute him, and also love sinners.'...These Jewish sayings ring like an echo of the words of Jesus in the Sermon on the Mount, 'Love your enemies' (Matt. 5:44)."

Seventh, "Love is the most superior way to God. On this way all high religions reach out toward the ultimate goal of divine infinity in which all finiteness finds its fulfillment, even though this goal may be visualized in different images. The Kingdom of God, heaven, paradise, the land of happiness (*sukhavati*), Brahmanirvana, and Parinirvana -- these are all but various names for one reality, the 'highest blessedness' (*paranam sukham*), as the Buddhists say." This is the ultimate answer to the question, "Is this all there is?" Religious thought says no. Believers feel there exists something more, a mystery that we can only glimpse now and then, but never fully understand in this life.

We concede that any list of unifying principles is bound to be incomplete or, at least, debatable. Perhaps there are similarities you would add to Heiler's list or some you would word differently or delete. The point however, is that all religious traditions seem to start from the same place (primordial tradition) and end in the same place (divine infinity). How they get there may look different and sound different, but substantively much is the same. Each tradition promotes some sort of sacrifice and service to neighbors, love for all creatures, reverence for the "holy," meditation or prayer, and some sense of the infinite.

Karen Armstrong told the story, in her new book <u>The Spiral Staircase</u>, of a group of pagans approaching Rabbi Hillel, a leading Pharisee who was a contemporary of Jesus, and told him that they would convert to Judaism if he could recite the whole of Jewish teaching while he stood on one leg. The rabbi stood on one leg and said, "Do not do unto others as you would not have done unto you. That is the Torah. The rest is commentary. Go and learn it." Many faiths have as part of their code of behavior this "Golden Rule." We saw a poster that illustrated this point beautifully. It listed eight different cultural versions of this core directive:

North American Indian: In the beginning were the instructions. They are to love and respect all living creatures and Mother Earth.

Hinduism: Do not to another what is disagreeable to yourself.

Judaism: What is hateful to you, do not to your fellowman.

Zoroastrian: That nature alone is good which shall not do unto another whatever is not good for its own self.

Baha'i Faith: Blessed is he who preferreth his brother before himself.

Islam: None of you is a believer until he desires for his brother what he desires for himself.

Christianity: Do unto others as you would have them do unto you.

Buddhism: Hurt not others in ways that you yourself would find harmful.

The beauty of all these instructions is that they deal with behavior. They all say that the manner in which we live our lives and behave toward each other is crucial to being a follower of God, by whatever name He is known. Like Rabbi Hillel said, "All the rest is commentary." These statements embody many of the seven principles outlined by Mr. Heiler. Religion seems to be more about right behavior than right belief when we examine the teachings with the perspective of Rabbi Hillel. Therefore it is no surprise that at the desired behavioral level we find striking similarities among the religions of the world. They all teach us that cruelty is wrong behavior and kindness is right behavior. We believe this foundation of unifying principles can lead to a new level of cooperation and respect among all religions. These are the bonds that unite us.

Discussion Questions

1) How do I explain the similarities amongst so many diverse religions, separated by space and time?

2) Is right behavior more important than right doctrine?

3) What are examples of right behavior?

4) How much does doctrine actually affect my daily behavior?

CHAPTER VIII

EMBRACING UNCERTAINTY

"I ain't much of a church man, Mark. Guess you might say I'm an agnostic. I don't know."

"There's a good bit of agnostic in all of us, Calamity. None of us knows much -- only enough to trust to reach out a hand in the dark."

Margaret Craven, in <u>I Heard The Owl Call My Name</u>

It strikes us as extremely unlikely that we can ever know with certainty God's thought processes. How can we possibly presume to totally relate to a supreme Creator who would endure billions of years of evolution of life until finally reaching the presumed endpoint of humans? For such a Being time is meaningless, yet for us of finite earthly existence it is of utmost importance. It seems presumptuous for any of us of limited time or breadth of experience and knowledge to declare ourselves in possession of God's true will. Do we buy into Rick Warren's notion that from the beginning of creation, God knew every detail of each of our lives, planned the universe, and orchestrated history? Are Phillip Gulley and James Mulholland correct in concluding that God will give grace to all -- it's God's choice, and we cannot reject it? Are "open theists" correct as they preach that God knows the past and present but not the future? Or does the Evangelical Theological Society have the inside track, along with Rick Warren, contending that God knows the past, present, and future? Or perhaps C.S. Lewis is correct in that God knows all, but only in the present, theorizing that time is of a different dimension for God and therefore grappling with questions of free will and God's omnipotence take on new meaning and, for C.S. Lewis, these questions then become easier with which to deal.

Conservative Anglicans, "knowing" God's wishes, oppose the election of a gay bishop who has faithfully dedicated his life to answering the call to make this a more compassionate and loving world. A high ranking general in the U.S. Army, stationed in Iraq, gives a speech proclaiming his god is bigger than the Muslim god and that the Muslim god is in fact an idol. Abortion foes, citing God on their side, murder physicians performing legal procedures as part of a private doctor-patient relationship. Muslim children are taught to hate Jews and westerners by fundamentalists invoking the name of God to support their agenda. Such proclamations are extreme examples of religious zealots using their scripture to support political agendas, and doing so with an attitude of superiority that is inflammatory. Attitudes of this sort do little to advance the agenda of parties on either side. To the contrary, emotional barriers are established which preclude worthwhile discussion. Is it not evident that the common theme here is that our concept of God's thoughts changes to conform to our own experience? Given that sacred scriptures themselves are products of not just divine influence but also human experience (if you accept our rationale in chapter IV), then it is reasonable to accept a degree of uncertainty relative to God's thoughts concerning all details. Even for those things that we believe we know in more absolute terms, can we fully appreciate all the factors contributing to such beliefs? We are but one small piece of an unfathomable whole. It is our nature and duty to share our opinions, but contrary to our nature, we need to be humble in so doing.

The practical experience of dealing with the dying patient serves to illustrate this point. As an intensivist Bill manages critically ill patients and is challenged with caring for patients and families during periods of futile care. Futile care from a physician perspective is care that it is expensive and emotionally traumatic for all involved once the ultimate outcome of death or unacceptable disability is virtually certain. Examples might include an octogenarian who develops an overwhelming infection (septic shock) resulting in multi-system organ failure (failure of kidneys, liver, lungs, and brain damage) or a young person with a ruptured brain aneurysm with resultant irreversible severe brain damage. Medical experience and literature confirm for the attending physician that it is appropriate medically and ethically to withdraw support for such patients and allow them to die. How and when to do so however is not always so obvious if one is empathizing with the struggle experienced by family members trying to make this decision not based upon a detached and rational medical perspective, but rather encumbered by emotions born of their personal relationship to the patient. Countless factors may contribute to decisions made by families that may seem irrational to their physician under such circumstances. But family members often just need some time to process through a difficult situation. It is the task of physicians to try to understand what will help these families heal in the aftermath of the passing of their loved one, not to twist their arms to understand that care is futile and then follow a cookbook approach to ending life. Delicate and emotionally charged issues such as this, much like debate amongst those passionate about religion, must be approached in a humble and empathetic manner with the realization that the emotional health of the grieving family member should be our focus, not promoting our "enlightened" medical opinion. As an experienced physician dealing with such matters on a regular basis the intensivist may *believe* he/she knows what is right for the patient *and* family, but only by truly listening to the family can one have any chance of actually *knowing* how to help them through the difficult process. It is in this same spirit of compassion whereby we find answers to the questions involving spirituality and religion. The answer is not always one that would be chosen by any single individual involved, but rather it is the best answer given the collective whole. Finding the answer that works requires dialogue and empathy. The answer will change depending on the parties involved.

We now find ourselves in the midst of global changes that give us cause to be optimistic for the plight of humanity despite tragedies commonplace in an imperfect world. The Nobel Peace Prize has been awarded to Shirin Ebadi, an Iranian woman, for her efforts to promote tolerance of religious and cultural differences. The "Arab Human Development Report 2003," written by a group of 23 Arab scholars, encourages a fresh look at critical problems previously not up for discussion: freedom, knowledge, and the status of women. As debate is encouraged, so positive change will eventually occur if sound principles of engagement are followed. Conservatives, wary of change and fearing secularism insults God, should be comforted by the realization that an omnipresent God can indeed be active in all moments, regardless of the spiritual or secular character of that moment. God's presence may not always be easy to discern, but for those with faith it can be seen manifest in ways not considered typically religious if one believes in a God without limits.

Ultimately, as ones who have not shared the faith experience of a personal God in the traditional sense described by many devout believers, we still find ourselves at times questioning how we fit into the current religious climate. There are so many unanswerable questions, yet for some the choice to believe, or not, is absolutely clear. They see things in black and white -- the restricted perspective of the analytical intellect directs the heart, or the passionate focus of the heartfelt faith convinces the mind -- and they easily make their choices. Many of us, however, see numerous shades of gray. There is a constant tug-of-war between heart and mind, and in the end we have to admit we are just not sure. On the most basic level the atheist and the passionate believer cannot both be right, yet each believes his/her own reasoning to be so sound as to be beyond questioning. Since the ultimate questions cannot be answered to the satisfaction of all, their conclusions cannot be *proven* to be wrong. For each, the other has used flawed reasoning of heart or mind to reach an improbable conclusion at best or is simply wrong if only the answer could be proven empirically. We have tried through the course of this book to give ample demonstration as to why neither position should be beyond questioning. Why does anyone choose one answer and is willing, in some cases, to literally die for the defense of principled reasoning knowing full well that one of the two must be wrong? It is important that we try to understand why such choices are made.

Let us assume the atheist is right -- there is no God. Additionally let us assume that the atheist personally knows this in a way truly beyond question, but let's assume further, and acknowledge this to be true based on the course of history, that theists would never be privy to the same awareness. Given these assumptions the atheist then has two choices. Comfortable with one's own knowledge, but unable to convince others who remain skeptical, the atheist may choose to remain above the discussion and essentially be disengaged so as to avoid involvement in spiritual matters. Or one can choose to accept that there is no way to *prove* to theists that they are wrong. With this acceptance comes another question. Can the atheist justify endorsing a positive role for religion in trying to reach the greater good? Can one in fact use the "self-serving delusion" to serve a cause for the good of all, in an all-inclusive way?

What if the theist is right? Is the monotheist's concept of a personal God the only possibility? Are we restricted to a choice between atheism and traditional monotheism? Considered from the broader perspective of personal and religious evolution, and not restricted by the notion of absolute authority, a third possibility warrants consideration. Perhaps God fulfills all parameters set forth by the monotheist's concept of a personal God, but at the same time may be something more, or simply something different, for those approaching spiritual matters from varying perspectives. If to be termed a "believer," we must conform to the traditional definition of a Christian, then we are decidedly agnostic, and just as passionate about our agnosticism as any devout believer, for having compared all the alternatives this is where our reality takes us. Are we to be faulted for the convictions of our beliefs that are a product of the spiritual journey we have shared in these pages? If we are to be designated agnostics by the traditionalist definition of Christianity, then we would favor the term "optimistic agnostics," for though we have found no absolute degree of certainty with respect to the traditional monotheist's concept of God and interpretation of scripture, we do in our minds and hearts believe in God. We now ask the traditionalist to revisit the question asked earlier: Is it a contradiction in terms to endorse the term Christian Pluralist? Is the definition of a Christian as determined by a group of men meeting in Nicea 1700 years ago the only definition to be applied in modern times? Should pluralists be embraced within the mainstream of Christian churches? Does the pluralist's concept of the religious Trinity further the cause of Jesus, or detract from it?

We don't think our uncertainty with respect to doctrinal issues translates into agnosticism, nor is it desirable to dodge the issue.

Rather, we feel it is important that all of us choose an answer to the question of God's existence. The reason for this we believe to be self-evident. Issues relating to God -- God's purported nature, thoughts, plans for humankind -- weigh heavily on the course of past, present, and future interactions of what has always been a diverse world, but one that now is becoming increasingly connected. For generations we have had the option to keep life simple and not address the matter of choice, feeling insulated from the ugliness of extreme positions, but we would suggest that none of us have ever truly been immune to the effects of religious conflict. It is too pervasive. It is particularly obvious in today's society given conflicts in the Middle East, Northern Ireland, Bosnia and throughout the globe. Disengagement is no longer a responsible option to choose.

The God to whom we relate, we believe, is the same God worshipped by Christians, Hindus, Jews, and Muslims, but this God is not limited to the personal relationship realm. We appreciate this type of relationship with God experienced by many but feel strongly that it is a mistake for any individuals to conclude that God is limited to relating to others only in this fashion. Some may sense or experience God's extended hand in a literal sense, but for many it is in a more ill-defined spiritual sense. The label of "optimistic agnostic" seemed to be a good descriptor of where we stood in our faith journeys prior to the study and introspection involved in formulating this book. Now, however, we sense at the root of our consciousness something that sparks in us a spirit of inquiry, a yearning for answers, a commitment to the journey and dialogue, out of which we find our moral compass. Is this spirit God? We cannot prove that in scientific terms, but our criteria for belief is not limited by such methodology. There is another type of reasoning, born of a feeling that emanates from the soul that makes sense not just because it works and is practical, but because once an individual has experienced this feeling it takes on a reality of its own. This experience is akin to the faith described by monotheists. At any given point in time these feelings are real but their origins should be acknowledged and they should be recognized as only probable truths. One cannot deny the realness of a first love, though in retrospect often misguided; or the palpable reality of anger, which may later be found to be misdirected or unwarranted. But until that additional information is received, and properly understood, the reality of the feeling stands unchallenged. We have a responsibility to challenge and critically evaluate our emotional responses and to be on guard for misperceptions, but this does not mean that all of our instincts and intuitions should be discarded as fanciful rationalizations. They still provide focus and grounding in our lives. All of us though may find ourselves subject to changing instincts, finding our probable truths in need of further consideration based upon evolving revelations of science, experience, and reason.

Scriptural inconsistencies and contradictions previously detracted from our study of the Christian Bible. Understood in the context described through this book, however, we now find in the message a God whom we believe to be real, though not necessarily one which must be defined in limited traditional terms. As ones who value the sincere experiences related by people of different faiths, we are indeed hopeful that this God is capable of speaking to all of us. For some, this may be in the form of a personal being, but for others it may just be a divine Spirit, or for others just a feeling, not requiring deification. Would God be insulted by our not glorifying the Creator in personal terms? We certainly hope not. That seems so petty when compared to so many life issues. We feel it is time to put aside the suffering promulgated by the competition for defining and understanding God in absolute terms. As Paul states in the book of Romans, "We know that suffering produces perseverance; perseverance, character; and character, hope. And hope does not disappoint us, because God has poured out His love into our hearts by the Holy Spirit, whom He has given us." We cannot help but be optimistic that we, as men and women of character and perseverance, will translate this hope and love into a world accepting of others without compromising our individual integrity. We challenge our religious leaders to understand and relate to those of us who, though we cannot accept all edicts of Scripture, do feel definite comfort and guidance from the God we sense in our lives. We need our leaders, as proposed by Albert Einstein, to "...avail themselves of those forces which are capable of cultivating the Good, the True, and the Beautiful in humanity itself." For many of us the primary force in this regard we believe is God, but a God untethered by societal, cultural, or religious traditions; a God present within all of us though difficult to define in terms acceptable to all; a "cosmic religious feeling" according to Einstein; the "Ground of Being" according to Bishop Spong; the "Holy Spirit" according to monotheists. This God is not limited by religious dogma, though such dogma, if not used for purposes of power or coercion, can be, and has been, useful for generations for those in search of spiritual growth.

Today's church must decide whether to reach out to that segment of its current membership who define their relationship with God in nontraditional terms or to the unchurched of similar mind. Being unchurched is not synonymous with being unspiritual. But these individuals do feel out of place, perhaps unwelcome, and certainly unfulfilled by traditional organized religion. They may yearn for a new church wherein they can better meet the demands of their sincere questions. The church structure provides the requisite organization to reach out to so many people in need. It would seem like such a waste to not utilize the structure already in place. To truly embrace those with an expanded or alternate understanding of God is one of our challenges to traditional religious leaders. The spiritual unchurched represent a huge untapped natural resource with potential to further the cause of the church itself. Synergies may be found if we are able to overcome the pride and fears that keep us from accepting faith experience in nontraditional ways.

A Christian physician addressing a medical student audience and speaking to the relative roles of science and religion as they affect the practice of medicine raised the alarm that we are a society so caught up by science that too frequently we veer astray from desired moral insights as we deal with ethical dilemmas accompanying the rapid pace of medical progress. To illustrate his point, he told the story of a scientist and a friend standing on the edge of a cliff looking into the distance where they see light emanating from a lighthouse. Asked by this friend what he sees, the scientist launches into an intellectual discourse about various properties of light such as wavelength and speed. Upon finishing he feels a definite sense of satisfaction for the triumph of science having elucidated the nature of light. His friend on the other hand, while acknowledging the validity of the scientist's observations, notes a message being sent in Morse code, "The cliff is about to crumble -- get off now or you will surely die!" The scientist's narrow focus had not allowed him to receive the true message. The physician lecturer makes his case that we should seek God's message and direction and behave in a morally responsible fashion, not blinded by the allure of progress for the sake of scientific progress alone. His point is valid, but is there more to the story? Perhaps upon reaching solid ground, had they both looked far to the left and right, well beyond the immediate light catching their eyes, they would have seen multiple other lighthouses each sending additional messages. Perhaps not all of the messages were intended for them; or maybe they were, but they needed others to help them interpret the message. Perhaps they needed to take a little time away from their scientific and theological discussions and actually visit with the people surrounding them, not to proselytize or enlighten them but rather just to be with them. Perhaps just being with the others would offer a means to new understanding previously unknowable to the "enlightened ones." Once we come down from our unstable precipice of religious pride and are on stable ground, secure with a foundation of a universal God unlimited by finite human experience, then our ears will be open to hear and our hearts free to receive the messages which surround us, heretofore under-appreciated, ignored, or denied.

James Hitchcock, Professor of History at St. Louis University, in his critique of the wildly popular and controversial The DaVinci Code, lambastes new age religiosity as inventing a system of belief which "...serves certain emotional needs and allows them to be 'religious' without submitting to any of the demands of faith." We hope our perspective will not be construed in this manner. Ours is a philosophy that submits to the demands of a faith that welcomes learning from people from all walks of life, a faith in a God that charges us with being one with a community larger than our current sphere of understanding and influence. We submit to a faith that demands that we work for justice for those less fortunate than ourselves and that we give of our time, talents, and resources generously in the pursuit of a life reflecting the lessons and values taught by Jesus, Mohammed, Buddha and others.

We talk so often of being tolerant of other viewpoints, but do we really value and learn from them? If in our schools and churches we just give passing acknowledgement of contributions of other cultures or religions without truly experiencing and understanding them, then it will remain "us" and "them." Haven't we learned anything from the plight of women, blacks, and the disabled in this country? It required twentieth century legislation and untold hardship of many tireless workers to ensure for these groups the basic rights provided for them by our constitution. True mutual respect however comes from living and working together, the shared experiences that build trust and empathy. It can't be legislated. We can legislate opportunity, but not choice. We can, and should, legislate opportunity for minorities regardless of race, religion, gender, or sexual orientation, but ultimately we need to teach our children from the earliest ages to celebrate diversity of individuals and religions. Look no further than the front page of the newspaper and read about the latest suicide bomber to see how effective early and consistent propaganda works. Why not apply the same principles, but instead of propagandizing hate messages or more insidiously promoting doctrinal superiority, instead teach the presence of universal common bonds and celebrate the diverse manner by which these commonalities are manifest. An increasingly diverse America recognized as the world leader of the global economy can ill afford to ignore the call for unification of those groups currently separated by issues of doctrine. If America aspires to be the world's moral leader, then it is a serious mistake to not address the insidious attitudes that result in a general making claim of a superior God or military personnel treating prisoners of war as subhuman species. We can continue theological and historical arguments indefinitely but given the discussions previously outlined concerning authority and truth we believe it is extremely unlikely there will ever be resolution. It is time to be practical. It is time to come down from the academic ivory tower and deal with real life problems that have solutions within our grasp, if we can value empathy over pride, diversity over doctrine, and acceptance over conversion.

The world is indeed changing, but our church is still relevant. We see it every day with people reaching out to others in need. But we plead for the barriers that limit our church's reach to be torn down. As we ask the traditionalist to embrace the concept of Christian Pluralism, consider this story shared by our pastor during a Sunday sermon. During WWII some American soldiers witnessed their dear friend, a Protestant, killed during combat. Wishing to provide him a proper burial they carried his body until they found a cemetery. It was a Roman Catholic burial ground. The priest who engaged them explained that the soldier could be buried there but would need to be just outside the fence since he wasn't Catholic. They left a small tombstone marking his site outside the fence and returned to their duties. Months later, with the war winding down, the friends returned to the site to pay their respects to their lost friend but were confused as they circled the fence but could not locate his burial marker. Soon they realized why. The night they had left after burying their friend, the priest, after being in prayer with God, had spent the entire night moving the fence. Their friend was now inside the fence.

We can envision no better means than to use our churches and schools to communicate a universal message that may effect real change. We are at a unique point in time with an opportunity awaiting us if only we embrace the change and accept being comfortable with the uncomfortable -- trusting in one's own beliefs while at the same time validating one's neighbor who holds to conflicting "truths." It is not enough though to just accept others in theory without translating thought into action. If set free by accepting the beliefs of others, then parents, teachers, clergy and political leaders must be empowered to work toward practical means of unifying people in conflict. Unencumbered by the need to fight religious battles defending the honor of any particular understanding of God, we should demand of our leaders that the bonds that unite us be strengthened while our collective differences, though celebrated by individuals in their own unique and personal spiritual manner, dissipate

Many mainstream Christian churches have contemporary services on Sunday mornings. These services are typically quite well attended and speak not only to the youth of the church but also to traditionalists. To some the lyrics of the rock music resonate in a way that brings special meaning to the day. For others it may be a contemporary drama, or a video clip from a current movie, or the sermon presented in a multimedia format, which speaks to a given individual. But the contemporary service has not supplanted the traditional service. Many cherish old familiar hymns, the choir adorned with traditional robes, the sermon deeply grounded in Old and New Testament scripture. The message can be successfully delivered in more than one way. The contemporary pluralist service offers the next generation of change. The concept can be applied to our schools as well as churches. We offer the following suggestions for those wishing to embrace religious diversity as we advocate:

1) Provide interfaith worship opportunities regularly during our mainstream contemporary services. Invite those who practice different faiths to share their experiences in a forum that obviously values cross-cultural exchange of ideas, not with the intent to convert, but to learn humbly side-by-side. Share our passions, but also our questions. Rejoice in the similarities that abound -- shared by our past, present, and future.

2) Bring the diversity dialogue to our schools beginning at the earliest ages. Allow our children to truly experience other cultures at an age where they have a chance to see others not as "them" but rather as just various parts of our whole; teach our children to be accepting; smother them with exposure to worlds otherwise never available to them. This instruction of course must be carried out in a prescribed non-biased manner that is embracing of all faiths, and includes a fair and consistent representation of the atheist and agnostic perspectives as well, for we have nothing to be gained from trying to force our perspective on others but everything to be gained from just engaging in nonjudgmental dialogue.

3) We will not overcome bigotry and intolerance unless we use all the tools at our disposal. We should not shy away from this discussion just because it is difficult. Certainly some will always be uncomfortable discussing matters involving sex, religion, or politics, but our churches and public school systems provide some of the most opportune venues to try to effect generational change. To overcome the "us " and "them" mentality will require intentional cross-cultural exchange over many generations.

This is an idea whose time has come. It is time to move the fence. The moderate middle -- pluralists from all walks of life -- need to start moving the fence posts one at a time.

DISCUSSION QUESTIONS

1) Does my uncertainty with respect to specific doctrine or knowledge of God's exact will lessen the value of traditional teachings for me?

2) Do I truly believe in God? If so, what form does God take in my mind? Should I expect others to visualize and experience God the same as me?

3) What if my church acknowledges some uncertainty too? Can my church remain relevant in a society that embraces relativism? How?

4) Would I like to see regular interfaith worship as part of our mainstream services?

5) Do I want our schools to incorporate the pluralist discussion and religious studies into their curricula to foster diversity?

6) Is doubt healthy?

EPILOGUE

There are peaks and valleys for first-time authors trying to tackle a subject like this. Our confidence in proceeding forward was, at times, shaky. Being highly interested and emotionally invested in the subject matter, but not academically expert, there is a good deal of unsettling vulnerability associated with the thought of actually going public with our thoughts. But eight months and two drafts into the writing of this book, we received from good friends a bulletin from a group called *Common Ground.* We found ourselves re-invigorated, validated, and excited about the possibility of our being able to make a meaningful contribution to the common cause. We subsequently have discovered numerous other websites espousing interfaith principles yet none seem to have attracted a major following to the point of having a significant impact on public policy or perceptions within mainstream churches. Ideas similar to ours have been proposed and debated for centuries yet have not found a coordinated widespread audience outside of certain academic or liberal circles. We hope, and sense, that the timing is right for the message now to reach and motivate lay people and clergy in search of a more satisfying and unifying role for religion in our society.

The dialogue is beautifully encouraged in an essay in Interreligious Insight (www.interreligiousinsight.org), the quarterly publication of *Common Ground, World Congress of Faiths,* and the *Interreligious Engagement Project.* This excerpt titled *Ethics and Globalization, the interreligious challenge* (April 2004) by John T. Pawlikowski, OSM (Professor of Social Ethics and Director of the Catholic-Jewish Studies Program at Catholic Theological Union Chicago, IL) concisely serves as a summary for that which we strive in writing this book:

> In conclusion, I strongly believe that religion today stands at a decisive turning point in this age of ever increasing globalization. Religious communities can withdraw into an isolated spirituality which cares little about what goes on beyond their self-defined borders. They can continue to be, as they have so often been in the past, sources of social tension rather than forces for social healing. But if religion follows such a path, it will squander its most precious gift -- the power to transform hatred into love, the power to turn indifference into concern -- that is at the heart of the Torah and Talmud, and the Christian gospel, the Qur'an and the teachings of the other great world religions. What will energize our enhanced technological capacity in directions that lead to social harmony rather than oblivion? Religion, I remain convinced, is very central to the answer to that question. It has the potential to penetrate hardened hearts in ways that secular ideology and mere technical competence cannot. It can combine

commitment and knowledge in ways that will overpower the forces of exploitation and destruction. We have seen outstanding examples of that power in the lives of Dr. Martin Luther King, Pope John XXIII, Nelson Mandela and Elie Wiesel.

But religion will not contribute in its fullness to global society unless it draws from the depths of its spiritual tradition, a tradition that is continually re-energized and refined in light of developing human understanding. Engagement with the world about us cannot become a substitute for a spirituality rooted in tradition. Rather, such engagement must always be the fruit of our spiritual tradition and, above all, it must be concretely embodied in the people of that tradition. Tradition does not reside first and foremost in texts and sacred books, as important as these remain. Rather we are the carriers of our respective traditions. We learn it in the classroom and in the library. It becomes the very fibre of our being in prayer and worship. We express it in our active concern and commitment to human dignity. None of these three elements of authentic religion can ever be separated from the rest without religion suffering a loss of its very soul. Become convinced that until the tradition is embodied in you it remains text rather than a force for human transformation.

As our collective traditions are "re-energized and refined in light of developing human understanding," we cannot help but conclude that most absolutes are too restrictive to have application across time and space. Relativism, we have tried to argue, is not a concept to disdain or discard as a threat to tradition or moral stability. The term "cultural Christian" need not be a derogatory term suggesting faith without substance. Rather, acceptance of relativism is the inescapable by-product of the developing human consciousness. Engaging in dialogue expands our collective understanding. The acceptance of relativism by traditionalists puts a human face on the church in a manner that serves to enhance its relevancy and can extend its reach and impact. We don't live in a time where most people believe that leaders of countries or churches are in direct communication with God and charged with handing out decrees that we are to follow as an obedient flock. Our leaders are not above the rest of us. We are all on spiritual journeys together but are endowed with cultural experiences and gifts of faith that necessarily differ from one another. When we learn to embrace these differences, the stage will be set to promote the dialogue that will indeed result in significant human and religious transformation.

When asked why they don't attend church any longer a group of recent college graduates shared some rather disconcerting impressions of contemporary Christianity. Christian leadership is seen as hypocritical in the exclusivity of its teachings. The concept of heaven vs. hell and the preaching of the justice/wrath of God manifest by natural disasters strike many of today's youth as incomprehensible and inconsistent with a concept of a loving God that they might care to endorse. When "Christian" schools ban children from attending because their parents are gay; when preachers proclaim from the pulpit that Hurricane Katrina was evidence of God's judgment of the decadent lifestyle of people of New Orleans; when "Christians" abuse or murder women or physicians at legal abortion clinics;

when evangelists such as Pat Robertson advocate assassination of world leaders; and the list goes on, is it any wonder that these youth lose sight of all the good that may be offered by Christianity or other organized religion? If they can find a sense of community amongst colleagues and friends, and at the same time be involved in efforts to promote social justice and humanitarian relief efforts without subjecting themselves to rigid, sometimes contradictory and confusing messages, why should they be involved with the church? We are certain this is a question with which church leaders wrestle on a daily basis as they see national and international trends documenting a decline in church attendance.

It is our hope that this book perhaps has provided some insight into why many become frustrated with the church and choose to leave organized religion. At the same time we hope it offers hope for a way to preserve and expand those aspects of our collective religious/spiritual lives that may serve to re-establish the religious experience to its appropriate place in our society. The church must not be used as an agent of political power or to oppress those with opposing ideologies, but it must be a vehicle for healing, a means to pull people into community, break down cultural barriers, eliminate prejudice born of ignorance or cultural tradition. Individual religions must recognize the complicated interweaving of those biases and traditions of the human experience that affect the origin, recording, translation, and interpretation of those doctrines or scripture decreed as "God-given." Only after recognizing and accepting this will our individual religions be successful in communicating the beauty of our traditions in a non-exclusive, non-superior fashion that will foster cooperation and community rather than competition.

Though we recognize that many readers will not agree with conclusions we have reached, we hope that it will be appreciated that we have gone through this process in a deliberate and thoughtful manner, and the conclusions reached are indeed rational for us, given our own biases. Furthermore, we hope that those that disagree do not lose sight of the underlying message that emphasizes compassionate caring for one's neighbor, whether friend or foe.

To engage you, the reader, as part of the process we ask that you consider a final few questions and respond to us at wcbjrc2003@gmail.com.

1) What part of the book spoke to you the most?

2) On a scale from 1-10, describing yourself as traditionalist vs. pluralist, what were you before reading this book? And after finishing it?

3) Do you believe the term "Christian Pluralist" to be a contradiction in terms?

4) Do you think the spiritually unchurched would want to be part of a traditional church embracing pluralism?

5) Would you support an expanded role for study of religious issues, from a pluralist perspective, in our schools?

6) Are you Republican, Democrat, or Independent?

7) Would you support a political candidate who is an acknowledged pluralist?

8) Your comments:

Thank you.
wcb/jrc

BIBLIOGRAPHY

Adler, Mortimer J. *Ten Philosophical Mistakes*, Macmillan, 1985.

Armstrong, Karen. *The Spiral Staircase*, Alfred A. Knopf, 2004.

Bhagavad Gita, A New Translation by Stephen Mitchell, Three Rivers Press, 2000.

Campbell, Joseph with Moyers, Bill. *The Power of Myth*, Doubleday, 1988

Cleary, Thomas. *The Essential Koran: The Heart of Islam*, HarperSanFrancisco, 1993.

Cohen, Shaye J. D. *From the Maccabees to the Mishnah*, Westminster, 1987.

Covey, Stephen. *The Seven Habits of Highly Effective People*, Simon and Schuster, 1989.

Dourley, John. *The Illness That We Are: A Jungian Critique of Christianity*, Inner City Books, 1984.

Einstein, Albert. *Ideas and Opinions*, Crown Publishers, Inc., 1954.

Gulley, Philip and Mulholland, James. *If Grace Is True: Why God Will Save Every Person*, HarperCollins, 2003.

Hollis, James. *The Middle Passage: From Misery to Meaning in Midlife*, Inner City Books, 1993.

Josephus. *The Jewish War, Books I-II*, Loeb Classical Library, 1927.

Kushner, Harold. *Who Needs God*, Simon and Schuster, 1989.

Lewis, C.S. *Mere Christianity*, Macmillan, 1943.

Maugham, Somerset. *The Razor's Edge*, Vintage International, 1972

Miles, Jack. *God, A Biography*, Vintage, 1996.

McDowell, Josh and Williams, Thomas. *In Search of Certainty*, Tyndale House Publishers, 2003.

Pagels, Elaine. *The Origin of Satan*, Vintage, 1995.

Pagels, Elaine. *Beyond Belief, The Secret Gospel of Thomas*, Random House, 2003.

Novak, Philip. *The World's Wisdom, Sacred Texts of the World's Religions*, HarperSanFrancisco, 1994.

Russell, Jeffrey Burton. *The Devil, Perceptions of Evil from Antiquity to Primitive Christianity*, Cornell University Press, 1981.

Sanders, E. P. *The Historical Figure of Jesus,* Penguin, 1993.

Smith, Huston. *The World's Religions*, HarperSanFrancisco, 1991.

Spong, John Shelby. *Why Christianity Must Change or Die*, HarperCollins, 1998.

Strobel, Lee. *The Case For Christ*, Zondervan Publishing House, 1998.

The Way Things Are, Conversations with Huston Smith on the Spiritual Life, edited by Phil Cousineau, University of California Press, 2003.

The New Oxford Annotated Bible, New Revised Standard Version, edited by Bruce M. Metzger and Roland E. Murphy, Oxford, 1991.

The Qur'an, Text, Translation and Commentary by Abdullah Yusuf Ali, Tahrike Tarsile Qur'an, Inc., 2002.

Warren, Rick. *The Purpose Driven Life*, Zondervan, 2002.

ABOUT THE AUTHORS

Bill Buffie grew up in Bloomington, Indiana and attended Northwestern University on a baseball scholarship where he was a senior co-captain and second team all Big Ten. After graduating Phi Beta Kappa from Northwestern in 1977 he entered medical school at Indiana University School of Medicine. Upon completing medical school with highest distinction (Alpha Omega Alpha), and then his residency in Internal Medicine, he became board certified in both Internal Medicine and Critical Care. He currently practices in Indianapolis where he is the CEO of a large multispecialty group while maintaining his full-time clinical practice as a hospitalist. He and his wife, Jo Ellen, have raised four children - Sean, Sarah, Claire, and Hannah - while attending Southport United Methodist Church. In his free time he enjoys gardening and playing tennis as well as travels with his family.

 John Charles was raised in Bedford, Indiana. He later served in the U.S. Air Force stationed in Europe before eventually graduating summa cum laude from the University of Southern Maine with a degree in history. He currently works as Assistant District Manager for an agency of the federal government. John, maintaining his interest in history and literature, is a voracious reader. He also enjoys college basketball and football and is a lifelong fan of the New York Yankees. He and his wife, Donna, also have been longstanding members of Southport United Methodist Church while raising their two sons, Adam and David. For nine years John has been active in the SUMC Disciple Bible Study program as both a pupil and teacher.

Printed in the United States
55819LVS00003BB/1-18